Pure Innocent Fun

Pure
Innocent
Fun ESSAYS

Ira Madison III

RANDOM HOUSE
NEW YORK

Published in the United States by Random House, an imprint and division of
Penguin Random House LLC, New York.

Random House and the House colophon are registered trademarks of
Penguin Random House LLC.

LIBRARY OF CONGRESS CATALOGING-IN-PUBLICATION DATA
Names: Madison, Ira, III, author.
Title: Pure innocent fun / Ira Madison III.
Description: New York, NY: Random House, 2025. |
Includes bibliographical references. |
Identifiers: LCCN 2024039652 (print) | LCCN 2024039653 (ebook) |
ISBN 9780593446188 (hardcover) | ISBN 9780593446195 (ebook)
Subjects: LCSH: Popular culture. | LCGFT: Essays.
Classification: LCC PS3613.A28447 P87 2025 (print) |
LCC PS3613.A28447 (ebook) | DDC 814/.6—dc23/eng/20240830
LC record available at https://lccn.loc.gov/2024039652
LC ebook record available at https://lccn.loc.gov/2024039653

Printed in the United States of America on acid-free paper

randomhousebooks.com

1st Printing

First Edition

For Bobbie

Whether we're talking about race or gender or class, popular culture is where the pedagogy is, it's where the learning is.

—BELL HOOKS

CULTURAL CRITICISM AND TRANSFORMATION (1997)

• • • • •

It's unfortunate that people can change something that was just pure innocent fun into drama.

—NENE LEAKES

THE REAL HOUSEWIVES OF ATLANTA (2008)

Contents

. . . . .

Introduction

On Chuck Klosterman

· · · · ·

My life has been a never-ending battle in defense of five British white men.

Those men are Jonny Buckland, Guy Berryman, Will Champion, Phil Harvey, and one household name—Chris Martin. Yes, ex–Mr. Gwyneth Paltrow himself. So why do I defend Chris Martin and his bandmates like I'm the Power Rangers defending the earth from Rita Repulsa? Because I really fucking love Coldplay. I didn't have to imagine my mom or younger sister admonishing me with a "boy, turn off that white music" if I dared to play Coldplay in the car. Coldplay was white music, but it was *also* uncool white music to my classmates at my predominantly white all-boys school, Milwaukee's Marquette University High School. That was my first realization that self-hate exists in every community—the phrase "It be your own people" could apply to white people, too.

To start, I used to think Coldplay sucked because one of my idols, Chuck Klosterman, hated them. No, he didn't just hate Coldplay; he referred to them as "absolutely the shittiest fucking band [he'd] ever heard in [his] entire fucking life" in his 2003 essay collection *Sex, Drugs, and Cocoa Puffs*. Described as a "low culture manifesto," the book features a collection of essays about music, film, and television and Klosterman's analysis of his Generation X cohorts. I discovered the book via the early-2000s teen soap *The O.C.* during an episode where Adam Brody's character, Seth Cohen, is seen reading Klosterman's book in his bedroom. At the time, I was a film-obsessed comic book nerd who read books instead of making friends at school, so Seth was one of my favorite TV characters.* Seth's tastes in pop culture led me to an obsession with Death Cab for Cutie, the Strokes, and, in turn, Klosterman's writing.

I bought the book based on the title and its connection to the *O.C.* It was through reading it that I experienced my first piece of cultural criticism (aside from obsessive viewings of *At the Movies*, the movie-review show hosted by Roger Ebert and Gene Siskel, and later Richard Roeper, after Siskel's death in 1999). While I did have my own completely embarrassing-to-read-as-an-adult newspaper column in high school, partly inspired by *At the Movies*, it was mostly movie reviews and gripes with high school theater productions that I wasn't cast in (these are confessions of being a teenage hater). I experienced some TV criticism on my favorite websites, BuffyGuide.com and Television Without Pity. Still, it wasn't until reading *Sex, Drugs, and Cocoa Puffs* that I realized you could write essays that weren't just movie reviews or recaps of TV shows. Not only had someone written a book about Britney Spears, *Saved by the Bell*, and Tom Cruise, but he had also written it as seriously as any term paper I'd ever been assigned.

While working at Borders and later Barnes & Noble, I began reading the book cover to cover every few weeks. In college in Chicago, I began reading *GQ, Esquire,* and other magazines Klo-

---

* As an adult, I realize Seth is the show's villain. Just like Xander Harris on *Buffy the Vampire Slayer.*

sterman had written for. As an adult, I discovered that Klosterman didn't invent pop culture criticism, but teenage me in the middle of Milwaukee didn't know that, and therefore I took everything that he wrote as a sacrament. If *Cosmo* was Elle Woods's Bible in *Legally Blonde*, my Bible was *Sex, Drugs, and Cocoa Puffs*. And if there was one thing I knew about Klosterman, it was that he *hates* Coldplay.

My classmates at Marquette felt the same way. If you've seen any film set in high school or survived the real thing yourself, then you know that teenagers are mushy brains waiting to be shaped by behaviors they observe and opinions they adopt. No pop culture take is formed in a vacuum, especially when you're in high school. It's why someone corny once coined the phrase "If your friends jumped off a bridge, would you jump too?" I mean, probably? Keith Raniere's cult NXIVM has got nothing on high school groupthink.

For instance, I learned about the existence of a band named Guster in high school. I do not know what Guster sounds like, and I've maybe listened to one song. But if you asked me who one of my favorite bands in high school was, I might say Guster, because everyone at Marquette loved Guster. It was better to agree with people than be the odd man out.

The one time I was almost forced to attend a concert of a band I'd never listened to was during Summerfest, a yearly music festival in Milwaukee. But Guster was playing at the same time as Ben Folds. I was a Ben Folds fan, because how could a high school student resist the psychic pull of lyrics like "Give me my money back, you bitch"? Ben Folds was one of my first entryways to white, angsty rock music that tapped into my high school anxieties. And thanks to Ben Folds, I never had to see Guster that summer and try to sing along to songs I didn't know the words to. High school involved a lot of lying about my taste in music.

. . .

One thing about Coldplay in the early 2000s is that their name was shorthand for shitty music. Coldplay made love songs, another thing considered uncool and "faggy," to quote the only adjective more popular among millennial teenage boys than "retarded." The only love songs that boys at Marquette knew were songs from the Beatles that they would play on acoustic guitar at parties. Of course, I say "songs," plural, as if they ever played any fucking song other than "Yesterday," but I digress. If you wanted to impress someone with your music taste, all it took was a quick dig about Chris Martin. Mind you, I loved Chris Martin. But I liked making my classmates laugh more. Coldplay's crime was they weren't just pop music. They were *popular* music, and a holdover from Gen X's culture of hating everything popular was that pop music was usually discussed with derision. Like the music of Britney Spears, which is often evaluated fondly in retrospective nostalgia. But I remember very well that liking Britney's music pre-"Toxic" was tantamount to being an Al-Qaeda terrorist. Long before sites like Pitchfork decided that pop music was a genre worthy of consideration, Britney was bubblegum pop. She was Kidz Bop. The anti–rebound sex anthem "Don't Go Knockin' on My Door" would like a word!

People criticized Britney and similar teen pop stars for not writing their own music. They were assumed to be lip-synching every performance. They made music for preteen girls. And more than being a punch line for the alleged unseriousness of her music, Britney Spears was also a punch line because she was blond and attractive and late-night hosts admit they wanted to fuck her (despite being a teenager at the time), but she wasn't a *"real"* artist like Alanis Morissette or Tori Amos. Not that men at the time gave an actual fuck about female rock artists, except when they were useful to slam pop music.

For instance, take Liz Phair, touted as a groundbreaking indie rock artist with her 1993 debut *Exile in Guyville*, only to be trashed by Pitchfork with an infamous zero-star review for her 2003 self-titled foray into pop, *Liz Phair*. In 2019, critic Matt LeMay apologized in a series of tweets for his "condescending and cringe" review and stated, "The idea that 'indie rock' and 'radio pop' are both cultural constructs? Languages to play with? Masks for an artist to try on? Yeah. I certainly did not get that. Liz Phair DID get that—way before many of us did." That's why, for Britney, it wasn't until "Toxic" debuted that the art kids at school, the arbiters of all music tastes, decided it was a great song, and other Britney songs were in regular rotation on people's playlists. The raucous production of "Toxic" was more aligned with something like the Prodigy's "Smack My Bitch Up" or Fatboy Slim's "Right Here, Right Now" than radio pop. It's extremely common for a millennial who once hated Britney to hit the dance floor excitedly when ". . . Baby One More Time" comes on.

So, I continued with the notion that Coldplay was the worst fucking band in the world until I found an ally, *another* idol of mine: R&B goddess Brandy. In 2004, she released the impeccable album *Afrodisiac*.* Her fourth studio album, *Afrodisiac* was mostly a collaboration with Timbaland, and it experimented with sounds more than her previous, traditional R&B albums. This was an album made for people who loved R&B but also fell in love with the bands that usually played on WB teen soap operas, from Bush to Aimee Mann to Portishead. One of my favorite tracks, "I Tried," samples "The Clansman" by heavy

---

* No skips!

metal group Iron Maiden, a band I'd only heard of in the pages of another of Klosterman's books, *Fargo Rock City*, which was an ode to an abundance of eighties rock bands I'd never heard of. It's ironic, then, that the opening verse of "I Tried" references Coldplay, who has very little in common with the heavy metal band Iron Maiden except that they're both British.

In "I Tried," Brandy sings that she wants to hear some Coldplay: "Especially that song where the man says, / 'Did I drive you away? I know what you'll say.'" The hilarity of Brandy referring to Chris Martin as simply "the man" aside, I began to think that if Brandy not only listened to Coldplay but was inspired enough by an Iron Maiden song to sample it on her album, then maybe there existed a middle ground where you could love saccharine pop songs as much as heavy metal. And so, I did what any college student in 2004 would do when they wanted to hear a new album. I downloaded Coldplay's *Parachutes* on LimeWire, which was a file-sharing service where you could pirate music. Well, and porn and movies, but only if you left your computer on overnight so it could download, because downloading anything longer than three minutes in those days took longer than binge-watching *Grey's Anatomy*.

By this time, I'd lost my copy of *Sex, Drugs, and Cocoa Puffs* to a college friend who never returned it, so I'd completely forgotten about my Coldplay vendetta by proxy. It took their debut album's fifth track, "Yellow," for me to become truly obsessed with Coldplay's propensity to describe love as sadness and longing. I was still closeted at this point, so Coldplay's kind of love, like having a crush on my straight best friend who didn't know I was gay, was the only kind of love I had ever experienced. This probably explains most of my adult romantic life and why I got hooked on daytime soap operas as a kid.

It's a common refrain online to pretend that Coldplay's performance at Super Bowl 50's halftime show was forgettable and that the only thing people remember about it is Beyoncé, clad in Black Panthers attire (no Wakanda), debuting "Formation" live. But as someone who became addicted to Coldplay, listening to them in bed on my fourth-generation iPod, the halftime show had the best of both worlds—a band I loved with a cosign from spiritual mother Beyoncé Giselle Knowles-Carter.[*] I love Chuck Klosterman, but baby, if Beyoncé loves Coldplay, then I love Coldplay.

---

[*] Google "Beyoncé and Chris Martin." She LOVES that man!

Pure Innocent Fun

WHITE BOYS

Saying you read *Playboy* magazine "for the articles" was a joke I heard often growing up. At the root of it was an acknowledgment that it was kind of shameful to look at pictures of naked women for pleasure, but when I first discovered porn, via vintage *Playboys* my gran's then-boyfriend Thomas used to hide in his favorite leather reclining chair, I actually *was* drawn in by the articles, and also the glamour of it all—the feathered hair, the campy lingerie, the visually striking photos. I was already obsessed with the divas on Gran's daytime TV shows, and now here were divas splayed out in centerfolds. The concept of the *Playboy* centerfold was prevalent in pop culture at the time. It was a thing that men looked at and teenage boys snuck behind their backs. It was lite pornography, something that turned on heterosexual boys. In the period of my adolescence, before I was willing to admit an attraction to other boys, I was convinced that my admiration for these centerfolds was an attraction to *Playboy*'s Playmates.

This is why I thought my obsession with the lead of my favorite TV series, *Buffy the Vampire Slayer*, was because I was *attracted* to her. And because of this, I got a subscription to *Teen People* magazine so I would never miss a cover with Sarah Michelle Gellar on it. As it turned out, she appeared on exactly one *Teen People* cover, the one I already had, but I discovered something else in the pages of the magazine that interested me even more than my beloved vampire slayer—a Calvin Klein ad.

In the early 2000s, Korn drummer David Silveria posed for a series of Calvin Klein ads that involved him wearing a pair of Dirty Denim shorts (knee-length jean shorts because those, unfortunately, had everyone in a choke hold then). In the ads, he's either lying on the ground of a desert or perched under the open hood of a car. Both ads feature him with frosted blond hair and an unfortunate black soul patch, but the most important part of these ads is that he is shirtless. And if the first piece of media to ever give me an erection as a kid was a sex scene in the 1981 Helen Mirren and Liam Neeson film *Excalibur*, the first one that made me realize I was gay was an ad of Silveria's muscled body lying on the ground in the masculine version of Kate Winslet's "draw me like one of your French girls" naked pose for Leonardo DiCaprio in *Titanic*.

Then, instead of sneaking away to read the *Playboy* magazines hidden in the recliner, I was returning to the same copy of *Teen People*. Eventually, I'd move on to Tommy Hilfiger model turned singer Tyrese's sex scene with Taraji P. Henson in the 2001 film *Baby Boy*, which I rewound several times. Soon after, Tom Cruise's 2002 *Vanity Fair* spread became my new Bible. The cover, a shirtless Cruise, immediately caught my attention during one of my weekly visits to Barnes & Noble at the Mayfair mall. Inside, a spread with two additional photos. In one, he flexes his biceps while gripping his tousled brown hair. In a second, his arm is behind his head, showing off his slightly hairy armpit. Since then, he has managed to remain one of our few lasting A-list movie stars—judging from the wild success of the Mission: Impossible franchise, the fact that *Top Gun: Maverick* seemingly brought a COVID-ravaged box office back to life, and his dizzying skydiving stunt at the 2024 Olympics closing ceremony. Given his long-standing association with the creepy cult of Scientology, this fame *has* to be in part thanks to that 2002 *Vanity Fair* spread.

Every recent generation has a moment when they fell in love with Tom Cruise. Gen Xers have Cruise in tighty-whities in *Risky Business* and his soft-core sex scene with Kelly McGillis in the original *Top Gun*. Millennials have him shouting "Show me the money!" at Cuba Gooding Jr. in *Jerry Maguire*. Gen Z has his death-defying stunts in recent *Mission: Impossible* films. For me, it's the *Vanilla Sky* era, when he divorced Nicole Kidman and began his rebrand as a hot nearly forty-year-old sex symbol. What was so enamoring about this white man with perfect teeth and beautiful hair? Well, for one, he had the biggest cosign of them all—Oprah.

I blame Oprah for many things, which I'll get to later in this book, but I'll say I'm *thankful* for the yearslong obsession with Cruise I've been given. It's hard out here for a Cruise fan. On the one hand, he's part of an evil cult. On the other, most of the films in his forty-year career are masterpieces, the majority of which belong in the Criterion Closet: *Jerry Maguire, Interview with the Vampire, Minority Report, The Color of Money, The Firm, Magnolia, Legend, Eyes Wide Shut*, every single Mission: Impossible film (except the second, which is possibly John Woo's worst American film, which I guess is my coming-out as a *Paycheck* fan, but I find it very hard to resist the charms of Ben Affleck and Uma Thurman), *Edge of Tomorrow, Collateral, Vanilla Sky, War of the Worlds, Tropic Thunder, American Made*, and maybe even *Knight and Day*—who's to say?

We can walk and chew gum at the same time. We don't have to lie that Cruise has never made a good film just because he maybe (probably) knows something about Shelly Miscavige's disappearance (this is absolutely a joke). Morally dubious people make great art all the time. Justin Timberlake's *Justified* is a great album, for instance. When Los Angeles was locked down due to COVID, I rewatched *Jerry Maguire* for the first time in years. I always knew it was a fantastic film (Cameron Crowe's best to me, but I know *Almost Famous* stans would riot if such an opinion were the general consensus), but I was unprepared for how utterly *moved* I would be. I'm sure it was in part from a lack of human contact during lockdown, but I truly uncontrollably sobbed on my couch watching not just the "you complete me" scene but also when Cuba Gooding Jr. survives what appears to be a life-threatening injury in the third act and embraces Cruise after his victory. Granted, I've sobbed at every Pixar movie since *WALL·E*, but that doesn't make my emotions any less real.

Unfortunately, there's just something mesmerizing about this short man who appears tall in his films and his perfect smile that seems to betray a near-psychotic evil brimming just beyond his porcelain veneers. For some, their unconscious uncoupling with Cruise began with Scientology and him leaping onto a couch on *The Oprah Winfrey Show*. On May 23, 2005, during an interview with Oprah where Cruise was supposed to be promoting Steven Spielberg's *War of the Worlds* remake, he spent the entire time talking about his new girlfriend, Katie Holmes, like your best friend does when they're drunk and just met a guy last night who they believe is the love of their life. (They'll never speak of this person again the next morning—or maybe that's just me.) This entire interview is key to understanding Oprah's ringleader, cultlike hold over Americans in the early 2000s and how big of a star Cruise was then. Before Cruise sets foot on Oprah's stage, she is commanding an audience of screaming, gasping women in near ecstasy. If you weren't a regular *Oprah* watcher in the show's heyday and only saw it through this clip, then you would be forgiven for mistaking the energy in the room as Cruise fandom. But actually, it was Oprah fandom. And since she's left the talk show behind and begun the "respectable elder" portion of her career, what's gone is the literal *insanity* that used to surround her. It was parodied constantly before Cruise's interview.

Here was a Black woman born into poverty in rural Mississippi who had become the most famous woman in media, perhaps one of the biggest celebrities in the world, and every day, you could tune in to see white women screaming in adulation at her presence. If it was the holiday season and she was handing out cars? You might think you were watching a human sacrifice in *Midsommar*. She addresses these women who have traveled to their version of Mecca in Chicago to see her and have just discovered that the guest on the show that day is Cruise. "Okay, you are all gonna have to *calm down*," Oprah says with a sly smile, almost toying with the audience. She did this often, whether it was teasing a guest or teasing the fact that they might get a new car (she became so famous for handing out cars to audience members that her screaming, "You get a car! You get a car!" has been forever ingrained into casual pop-culture slang). "Y'all are gonna have to calm yourselves or you won't make it through the hour, I'm telling you, because . . ." And then she said, with her usual delivery of a deep, drawn-out shout, "He's in the building!"

The camera cuts to white women screaming, gasping for air, hugging one another through tears like an alternate reality in which Hillary Clinton won the presidency in 2016. Oprah has everyone in the audience take a Lamaze-class deep breath and then gets on with the business of introducing Cruise, but not before teasing them all once more by bringing up his "new love" and saying, "I must say, I was hanging out with the new couple the other day . . . at my Legends Ball." One thing Oprah is really good at is name-dropping her celebrity friends, but it always comes back to Oprah! Forget *Madame Web*; it's Oprah who connects them all.

"Please welcome Tom Cruise," she bellows, which prompts a giddy, smiling Cruise to walk out from backstage and embrace Oprah sweetly. Before the interview even begins, he's unable to stop grinning at the insane reception he's getting. "Is it like this every day here?" he asks Oprah, which, in part, is a joke about how whipped up the audience is for his presence, but also, no shade, the audience *was* like that every fucking day. It takes about two minutes before the interview even begins; the audience screams in hysterics every time Cruise utters a single word. But when he does speak, he starts to sound increasingly unhinged until he starts talking about Katie Holmes, and then all the wheels come entirely off. "I'm in love," he says, and starts describing his love for her like someone who's been ripping lines at an after-party for five hours and has trapped you in a conversation. The audience shrieked every time he smiled, every time he mentioned Katie Holmes's name, every time he went into his rehearsed spiel.

One of the oddest moments is when Cruise describes how he met Holmes. I know that dating for celebrities is weird. You can't mingle with anyone who isn't a celebrity, TBH, so dating feels a lot like work. But Cruise's first interaction with Holmes feels like he ordered her to his home via DoorDash. And yet, he can barely explain *why* he's interested in Holmes. He says he'd seen her work before, that she was so incredibly talented that he had to meet her. Listen, I love Katie Holmes as much as the next person, but I doubt this man was watching *Dawson's Creek* and *Disturbing Behavior*.

At one point, a man in the audience asks Cruise a question,

and he's *stunned* that there's a man in the audience. The idea that a man would show up at Oprah's show to see him talking about *War of the Worlds* is bewildering to him, which is odd because that's the primary audience for his films. But because he's there to mainly talk about his relationship with Holmes, he seems to have forgotten all about the movie he's there to promote. He can't even pretend to care about the other Tom Cruise who shows up—a man who shares the same name as him. It's the kind of silly thing you'd see on TV all the time back then, but Cruise is more interested in running backstage and grabbing Holmes and forcing her to face the audience.

It wasn't until after the interview that Cruise realized he'd made a misstep, but Oprah noticed it early on. She asks if he's been sleeping when he first leaps onto the couch. It's an innocuous question, and there are a variety of answers, but it's telling that he doesn't blame the film shoot or anything else that could add to his strenuous schedule. Instead, he discusses being up all night eating Garrett popcorn and Giordano's pizza with Holmes. All excellent choices, BTW, because as I've always said, the best pizza is from Chicago. Not a joke; just a fact.

Returning to my point about Cruise's erratic behavior not just being a symptom of this audience, Oprah brings up how energetic he was recently at her Legends Ball. In a light way, it's like she's telling him, "Your crazy white ass embarrassed me in front of all these Black folks." But Tina Turner beckoned him to her table, so all was forgiven. She also mentions how he's utterly puzzled by the idea of other humans. Like when they're at dinner, he'll be inquiring if the man pouring the water likes his job and how his day is going. "I love people—not *that* much," Oprah says.

If anything, the interview is much more revealing about who Oprah was then in this moment. Cruise became a brief (well, not thaaaat brief) punch line, but it didn't affect his career in the long run. Maybe it made him retreat into comfortable action movies and stop trying to win Oscars. Cruise *did*, at one point, consider himself an *actor*. After this, he seemed resigned to being a movie star. And if he was gonna be a movie *star*, then he was gonna be the biggest fucking movie star on the planet.

Oprah, on the other hand, has retreated from the circus she used to ringlead. Now we associate Oprah with presidential endorsements, soft sweaters, and residing on pergolas, like the one lent to her for her Harry-and-Meghan sit-down by a Montecito neighbor. (She allegedly used Rob Lowe's home, according to Deuxmoi.) She has recognized that her interview skills are much stronger without a breathless studio audience. She has always commanded star power in her interviews, but as the idea of megastars fades from the public consciousness, who is left for Oprah to even *have* sit-downs with, besides royalty? After all, isn't she royalty herself?

The most interesting thing about this interview is that I cannot imagine Oprah conducting anything like it ever again. She don't love these hoes like that. I don't think she ever did. "You're gone," she says repeatedly through a smile while also realizing that Cruise might have lost his grip on reality while *also* realizing this episode was going to be ratings gold. When Cruise runs backstage to march Holmes out, and they're clinging together like lovesick teenagers, it was one of the most shocking displays I'd seen from a celebrity on live TV. And this was coming only a few years after I'd watched Mariah Carey, during an emotionally and physically taxing moment in her career, make a surprise appearance on MTV's *Total Request Live* with an ice cream cart and do a striptease, removing an oversize "Loverboy" shirt (promoting her new single) to reveal a tank top and gold hot pants underneath.

But I'd argue that any true fan of Cruise has always seen him for what he is—a soulless cipher skilled at mimicking human emotion. I was born in the eighties, so my introduction to Cruise wasn't via watchable garbage like *Cocktail*. He has an affable persona in films like that or *Losin' It*, but he's the epitome of a young, charismatic white male plucked out of obscurity by Hollywood to churn into a star of the moment. The eighties were full of those archetypes who don't have the brooding melancholy of Hollywood's Golden Age stars or the cynical realism of those who starred in Martin Scorsese, Sidney Lumet, and Sydney Pollack films in the seventies—the Rob Lowes, Emilio Estevezes, Corey Feldmans.

In a world where Cruise isn't introduced to Scientology, he'd have still been one of the coolest celebs of the eighties (there's nothing but swag in a photo of him and Keith Haring in the back seat of a limo en route to Madonna's wedding to Sean Penn) and would surely have an equally successful Hollywood career. Though instead of the multimillion-dollar Mission: Impossible franchise, he'd probably be the current star of a prestige cable TV drama. But for Cruise to not only join Scientology but to also become their poster child for success (in a way that John Travolta couldn't even accomplish without becoming a punch line), there had to be some part of him that enjoyed the darkness's seduction.

Ever since then, Cruise has been kinda like Dexter. *Dexter* was a show about a serial killer attempting to be human. Just like Dexter methodically monologues about how he should act amongst people to seem "normal," Cruise approximates human behavior in a way that makes you think he's *learning* how humans interact with one another, not merely observing and deciphering it like most actors. But he's at his most sublime when he's approximating how *we* perceive him. He's playing his younger self in *Jerry Maguire*. He's playing his most malevolent self in *Magnolia*. In *Mission: Impossible,* he's truly attempting to push the human body to its breaking point. And yet, he comes off as a very endearing and lovable robot. He's the flawed hero humans have been writing about since the *Iliad*. When his corporeal form becomes dust, the epic story of how Thomas Mapother IV, born July 3, 1962, in Syracuse, New York, became Tom Cruise should be told for generations.

Not every white boy I became enamored with needed a co-sign from American royalty like Oprah. The very first one, Steven, was the one white boy who only hung out with Black kids in middle school. My education until high school was in largely nonwhite environments, so Samuel Morse Middle School was predominantly Black. The Black girls at school loved Steven. He dated several of them over the course of three years, and he was what we lovingly referred to as a "wigga," which means exactly what you think it means—"white nigga"—which would be think-pieced to death if it resurfaced as a popular phrase now. Still, it was an extremely useful phrase for people like Steven (and Eminem) in the late nineties.

Steven was also the first person to defend me on two separate occasions from the most evil girl I'd known until I saw the 2009 film *Orphan*. Gina, a classmate with some inexplicable chip on her shoulder, first asked, "What are you, gay?" when I admitted I was listening to an Aaliyah album at school—the *Romeo Must Die* soundtrack, to be precise, but I consider that to be Aaliyah's third studio album. Steven piped up with the defense "Maybe Ira just thinks she's hot." Nowhere in an adult world of logic would that fly, but when the cool boy in your grade says anything, it's always accepted as fact.

The second time he came to my defense was when Gina *insisted* I was a faggot on the school bus. This was a lose-lose situation, because how do you respond to a girl who's techni-cally very much right (maybe I was gaslighting *her*?) but being a bitch about it? If it were a boy, I'd have just hit him,[*] but as I was left to sputter a response, the only thing that came out of my mouth was "Maybe I am!" Which was exactly *not* the correct response, and at this point, Steven clearly must've known I was gay, given how I used every opportunity at school to talk to him and he often found me staring into his piercing blue eyes in the middle of class. But he once again came to my defense and said, "Man, Ira's the funniest person in class. He's gonna be a come-dian someday." I hope Steven knows that I *am* considered funny by some people (maybe even you), but given his incredibly common name, I have never been able to find him on social media in my adult life. I'll never know if he's grown into a hot-ter version of the teenager I remember, who's still cool and has helped some other gay person feel better about themselves. Or maybe he was defending me from accusations that I was gay because *he* was also gay, and one day the big city will become too much for me and I'll quit my job and return to my small town (let's pretend Milwaukee is a small town), where he'll fall in love with me when I run into him while working as a barista at a Black-owned bookstore/jazz café.

When I departed the bus that afternoon, the bus driver, a woman who seemed to like me but had chosen very much not to intervene in my bullying that day, told me in a serious tone, "Don't tell people you're gay. Even if you are." Honestly, great advice.

Further fueling the rumors that Ira might be gay was the fact that Mom and Gran decided that because I was a "good

---

[*] I probably would not have. I've been in exactly two fights, both in swimming pools, and I nearly drowned each time.

student," which, at Morse, mostly meant I had an above-average reading level and could passably solve math problems on tests by studying the morning of on the bus, I was to attend Marquette University High School, an all-white, all-boys Jesuit high school. The concept of an all-boys school in Milwaukee in the year 2000 meant that everyone at the school was gay. Not only did I have to endure serious questions as to whether I was going to be afraid of showering with these alleged gays in high school—as if I, a person who became fat the summer before middle school, had *ever* showered in the presence of another person in a school setting—but I also learned that because Marquette was number one in most state athletics, other schools frequently taunted the players at games with cheers that involved the actual word "faggot" in many of them—a thing that no school official seemed to care about. This, of course, meant that I would not be attending Rufus King High School with any of my friends, which might as well have been an HBCU compared to Marquette.

I never had the best attitude growing up, especially compared to my perfect-grades, beloved-by-our-mother, soccer-team-champion sister. Still, my surly teenage years fully emerged once I was enrolled at Marquette. I wasn't just unenthused about the prospect of spending my time at a school with no friends. I had taken on a decidedly anti-Marquette approach at orientation day, which I attended with Gran. The school, endowed with the money of a lot of rich white parents, was giving Xavier's School for Gifted Youngsters, but the only superpower seemed to be campaigning for George W. Bush and Dick Cheney. I'd never even given a thought to politics before, aside from the occasional Bill Clinton–and–Monica Lewinsky joke on late-night TV, but at Marquette, I was suddenly very aware that most of the students there had Bush–Cheney bumper stickers on the Lexuses, Audis, and BMWs that populated the student parking lot.

In her best way of encouraging me to stop annoying the fuck out of her, Gran's advice was "Why can't you be like these white boys who are nice to their parents?" Instruction to be like the white boys at school felt like a mantra seared into my brain for the next four years that I actively rebelled against, and it brought me delight when I realized the facade that most of these kids had adopted in front of their parents.

Here's the thing about a school full of privileged white male teenagers: When you watch a show like *Gossip Girl*, it might seem far-fetched that Chuck Bass gets away with all the things he does. But it's a lot more realistic after four years at a high school with scandals like art students printing counterfeit money and using it in the cafeteria, a student getting grilled by the FBI for allegedly attempting to blow up our social studies teacher and who knows who else, or two students building a grow house in an attic and getting busted because they were also serially burglarizing homes.

One of those students who burglarized homes, Cliff, is also one of the students who planned to blow up our social studies teacher. He and his partner in crime, Pulaski, the Leopold to his Loeb, were also the two who took on the role of terrorizing me like Gina my first week of school by paying a freshman named Max a quarter (a quarter!!! Aim higher!) to ask me in front of everyone at a school fundraiser if I was gay.* Unlike on the bus in middle school, I did not sputter and stupidly admit to my gayness this time. I told everyone involved to fuck off.

---

* That student, Max, became one of my best friends in high school and my roommate in college, and I was in his wedding. Naturally, I bring up the quarter incident every chance I get.

Similar to how lovesick teenagers read *Romeo and Juliet* and forget about the fact that the lovers end up very dead in the end, I read *Julius Caesar* freshman year, and my way of becoming liked at school was to amass power (me forgetting that everyone stabs Caesar to death), which of course meant that being the entertainment editor with a regular pop-culture column wasn't enough for me. One thing I knew about Marquette was that we were really good at athletics. Another thing I know is I suck at sports. So instead, I became the sports editor of the *Marquette Flambeau* newspaper.

For like, six months at most. By the way, during this period, we released about one and a half issues. I am constantly amazed by TV series that depict high schools with the ability to produce a daily newspaper, because our high school couldn't even publish our newspaper *monthly*. Every two to three months was a more reasonable goal. You'd think a school with all the resources in the world would be able to pump money into the production of a school newspaper, but in retrospect, the fact that our Catholic, conservative-leaning school had a practically dismantled journalism enterprise was a precursor to the world we're currently living in. Or, at least, it should've prepared me for most of the media outlets I worked for as an adult crumbling out of existence.

Throughout my brief tenure as newspaper editor, I had to pay more attention to the student athletes, and it was during this time that I encountered the second most important wigga in my life—Stuart ("Stu," for short). Stu was a star basketball and football player (we give far too much power to teenage boys who are good at more than one sport) who I briefly thought might be pulling an *Imitation of Life* since his skin wasn't as Casper-like as the rest of my classmates'. But it just turned out he was a very tall Irish kid who liked to tan. Aside from playing basketball and liking hip-hop, however, Stu was also curiously into *The O.C.* If I were thinking of immediate markers to signify to my classmates that I was a faggot, loving a teen soap opera on Fox would've probably been high on the list.

Still, what you should know about *The O.C.* is that straight guys liked it. Even straight guys who played *sports* liked it. This is likely because *The O.C.* debuted in the summer of 2003, meaning that high school students with absolutely nothing to do but drink in their parents' basements and have sex had the free time on Thursday nights to watch it. Presumably with their girlfriends who they had sex with. Following Fox's model of debuting seasons of *Beverly Hills, 90210* and *Melrose Place* in the summer so that kids could get hooked without the burden of school, the show debuted to 7.46 million viewers and continued to grow each week. Seven episodes in the series aired before classes started, and it amassed nine million weekly viewers.

The series had direct appeal for straight boys in the way that *Dallas* did in the eighties over *Dynasty*, which was purely for women and gay men. The genre of a "masculine" soap is especially intriguing to me because while it has all the trappings of a regular soap that focuses on female protagonists, it instead centers on male protagonists who go through all the same relationship drama and turmoil that come with soaps.

Ryan Atwood, played by Ben McKenzie, is a troubled teen from the wrong side of town (mostly, it means Mexicans live on this side of the town rather than working for white people, and every scene set in the bad side of town had a sepia Instagram filter years before Instagram existed) who is adopted by the Cohens, a wealthy family in Orange County, California. For

Ryan, being troubled means that he often gets into fistfights and he's not big on words and certainly doesn't fit in with the Orange County crowd, essentially making him a modern Clint Eastwood type. He appealed to normal American teenage boys who related to him, and in the case of the rich kids at my high school, they just thought he was cool.

Unlike Seth Cohen, his surrogate brother on the series. Seth is a nerd who is into movies and indie bands, and while he's great comic relief, if the series had been focused on him, I doubt it would have done as well with teenage boys. *Dawson's Creek* was another successful teen show that focused on a male lead, but Dawson was basically a Seth Cohen type, a sexless nerd who was extremely annoying. And while that type of man makes the kinds of movies that teenage boys love to watch, they don't want to *be* those men. You want to watch Tarantino films, but you don't want to *be* Tarantino.

The O.C. was all anyone wanted to talk about once we returned from summer break, and it was one of the big things I bonded with Stu over. There is something amusing about hearing teenage boys discuss the intricate plotlines of a soap opera with the same fervor they'd later discuss storylines on *Game of Thrones* in adulthood (also a masculine soap, but because it has a lot of blood and tits). For two years, discussing *The O.C.* was the easiest form of small talk for me to use with straight men, especially once I got to college and was thrust into a dorm floor with straight boys, where it was even harder to pretend I wasn't gay. But at least three straight guys on my floor had the season-one DVD box set of *The O.C.**

Cultural interest in *The O.C.* would eventually die down, as

---

* One of said boys made a joke about me being gay, and for the first time, I retaliated—I stole his *O.C.* box set.

its ratings dipped to half its season-one audience by season three. The argument could be made that most soap operas can't sustain that much of an audience for multiple seasons, but the problem with *The O.C.* is really that it stopped being cool and started being a soap. Once Ryan became acclimated to life in Orange County, he was pretty much indistinguishable from the rest of the characters on the show, and what used to be a clever satire of soap opera trappings and clichés now relied on clichés to come up with subsequent stories. Watching Ryan constantly lose his girlfriend, Marissa, to interlopers made him uncool and kind of a loser, and nobody signed on to watch a show about a loser.*

The beauty of nostalgia, however, is that most people forget the things that they hated about something they love, and if you ask any millennial what they think about *The O.C.*, they'll solely remember it in broad brushstrokes as one of their favorite TV shows. They won't remember that they stopped watching it when it got boring. This romanticization phenomenon is also why websites like BuzzFeed thrive, because it only reminds you of the beautiful parts of nostalgia. One thing the pandemic managed to do is satisfy a lot of people's nostalgia cravings. With so much time to do nothing, my friends and I revisited *The O.C.*, and all our wonderful memories of one of our favorite shows came flooding back. Unfortunately, we all quit watching the show around the exact time we quit watching the show in the early aughts.

I think nostalgia works best when you don't look back like Orpheus, because my memories of *The O.C.* also made me look

---

* Season four is a huge improvement on the previous two seasons because the series abandoned all sense of reality and became a parody of not just soaps but also of itself. It's incredibly funny and underrated, but nobody watched it and the show got canceled.

up Stu, the athlete at school I had a crush on, and I was quickly met with the fact that he follows Ben Shapiro and other right-wing nutjobs online. That's the thing about the term "wigga." It still has the word "white" in it, and chances are a white man is going to let you down.

> Till next time, take care of yourself and each other.
> —JERRY SPRINGER (1991–2018)

· · · · ·

NO WATCHING *THE SIMPSONS*

A friend recently wondered why actual teenagers are watching *Euphoria*, as if that's not the intended audience for the series about drug-addicted, promiscuous hot adults playing teenagers, with three good scenes of material each season crafted for Zendaya to win Emmys and Jacob Elordi to pout pornographically. I reminded my friend that when *we* were teenagers, we were also watching racy HBO series like *Sex and the City* and *The Sopranos*.

Though I lived with Gran, when I visited Mom on some weekends, I would take full advantage of the fact that she had the premium networks Gran didn't. Not that she spent her own money on them. Back then, everyone had a guy in the neighborhood who'd sell you cable with "all the channels" for a few extra bucks. Mom and I, despite our lack of sitcom-level bonding with one another as mother and son, at least bonded over Carrie Bradshaw's neurotic love woes and Tony Soprano's therapy sessions. However, for reasons that elude me now, we did not have HBO during my senior year of high school and the final season of *Sex and the City*, so I didn't get to finish the series until a year later, when I ordered a complete series box set off eBay from someone in Japan who'd burned the entire series onto DVDs. Every episode had Japanese subtitles.

Max, one of my best friends in high school who later became a college roommate, was a TV-obsessive like me and had
the money to pay for an HBO subscription, so we routinely
watched *The Sopranos* every Sunday until I spent the summer
between my junior and senior years in New York and managed
to miss the final season of *that* series too. I have, to this day, not
watched the final season of *The Sopranos*, and two failed attempts to rewatch the entire series during a pandemic later
(due to my general ADHD and hatred for that Christopher Co-
lumbus episode), I have come to terms with the fact that I probably never will.

This is all to say that my mother had a healthy acceptance
of her son consuming violence and sexual content on TV. For
instance, I could freely watch films like *New Jack City* (which
should be in the crime-film canon with *Goodfellas* and *Scarface*)
and *Belly* (horrible, yet one of the best films ever). When it
came to sex, her only qualm was that for a prolonged sex scene
in a movie, I was required to cover my eyes, a common practice
during *The Young and the Restless*, which aired after *The Price Is
Right* and introduced me to the phrase "make love" as romantic
leads Nicholas and Sharon Newman had multi-sequence sex
scenes set to horny jazz music. Which makes the shows I wasn't
allowed to watch odder.

Granted, these restrictions were at Gran's behest, not Mom's.
As a rule, Gran did not even have liquor in her home, and I always feel weird when I do visit Milwaukee and chill a bottle of
wine in a fridge that hasn't seen another alcoholic beverage
since a Clinton-era family cookout. But on Sundays, Gran's boyfriend Thomas would watch *The Simpsons* and *The X-Files*, and
Gran did *not* like *The Simpsons*. Maybe it was since the show
often made fun of religion, which is not to say that we were a

particularly religious family. I was raised Baptist, and on occasion we did attend church to praise capital H-I-M, but once I decided I didn't want to go on Sundays anymore, no one put up a fight. My family learned early on that it was easier not to exhaust themselves trying to convince me to do something I didn't want to do. There's also the possibility Gran just didn't like the damn show.

Whatever the case, I do recall not being allowed to watch *The Simpsons* and never seeing a full episode of the series until high school, when I caught episodes in after-school-hours syndication. I suspect the core of most parents' dislike of *The Simpsons* was due to Bart Simpson. Bart, a flippant and dismissive asshole, despite not being intended as such, was the ostensible lead of the series in the nineties, thanks to a slew of merchandise produced with his image. In spite of my never having seen the series, Bart was ubiquitous to me, much in the same way *Mad Men* never had more than five million viewers for a single episode, yet most Americans can accurately identify the time period and fashion associated with *Mad Men*. Even Banana Republic started selling clothing in tandem with marketing the series to people who didn't know who the hell Don Draper was.

Bart Simpson could be found on a variety of merchandise, from lunch boxes to comic books, but it was the T-shirts that I coveted the most—drawings of Bart on oversize white T-shirts with catchphrases like "Eat my shorts," "Don't have a cow, man," and, my personal favorite, "I'm Bart Simpson. Who the hell are you?" Mom still said "*H-E*–double hockey sticks" around me in an effort to keep me from swearing, so the chances of me wearing a Bart shirt in her presence was like a snowball's in . . . You get it. I had to settle for a windbreaker with the Tasmanian Devil on it, an animated character from the Looney Tunes[*] franchise who is probably a complete "huh?" to anyone Gen Z and younger. Looney Tunes in current popular culture is pretty much nonexistent, save for *Space Jam: A New Legacy*, which *Forbes* dubbed "a successful disappointment" because it lacked the boffo box office that animated films usually garner, probably because kids have no brand recognition of those nearly-a-century-old cartoons anymore. Also, the reviews sucked.

Bart Simpson is an underachieving slacker, which is the sort of TV character seen as a horrible influence on children. And while the series was never actually *for* children, it was animated, which was still shorthand for "for kids" before the advent of things like Adult Swim or the United States' discovery of anime. Fox certainly made a shit ton of money marketing the show to children, even if their parents forbade them from watching it.

In January 1992, when the culture wars involved raunchy TV shows and rap music threatening white America's two-state solution,[†] George H. W. Bush employed an oft-used Republican sleight of hand trick: turn a piece of pop-culture entertainment into a conservative talking point on American values. In Bush's State of the Union address that year, he said, "We are going to keep on trying to strengthen the American family to make American families a lot more like the Waltons and lot less like the Simpsons."

I have never seen more than one episode of *The Waltons*, a drama series that aired from 1972 to 1981 about a family in

---

[*] An animated franchise led by Bugs Bunny, a scheming, cross-dressing rabbit, and a host of other characters like Elmer Fudd, a hick who, in present day, either would have voted MAGA or come out of the closet, or both, and Tweety, a very cute canary who is also a cunt.

[†] The suburbs.

rural Virginia during the Great Depression, which makes it apt for Republicans waxing philosophically about "American values" and bootstraps or what the fuck ever, even though the Depression was a shit time for Americans.

Never mind that *The Simpsons* was a literal representation of a nuclear family: patriarch Homer Simpson worked a blue-collar job; his wife, Marge, was a stay-at-home mom; and they had three kids—Bart, Lisa, and Maggie. The Simpsons are kinda the ideal American family unit conservatives constantly bemoan isn't represented on TV in 2025. But in 1992, foul-mouthed Bart Simpson was a harbinger of kids who would learn to talk back to their own (Republican) parents and vote the way underachieving slackers traditionally do (Democrat). Ahead of the series' 1993 season, the show *did* transition Homer to the de facto series lead over Bart, but that's in large part due to showrunner David Mirkin's idea that the series should be "more emotional and bigger in scope,"* an impossibility when, as an animated character, Bart was never going to age. But by the time *The Simpsons* matured into Homer-centric stories, Bush had already lost his rebid for the presidency to Bill Clinton.

The media censorship of the eighties was slowly eroding on TV, from *The Simpsons* to other series like *Married . . . with Children*, which starred Ed O'Neill as the breast-ogling, feminist-hating shoe-salesman patriarch of the Bundy family. The show was a crass, hilarious precursor to series like *It's Always Sunny in Philadelphia* and lasted for eleven seasons on Fox. TV's pivot to vulgarity also spilled into daytime TV. If the mischievous, anti-family-values Bart Simpson had had a human equivalent on TV, it was Jerry Springer.

---

* As told to the *New York Post* in 2007.

Jerry Springer, the self-dubbed "ringmaster" of daytime TV, hosted *Jerry Springer*, a daytime talk show that debuted in 1991 with an initial focus on political issues, as Springer began his career as a campaign adviser for Robert F. Kennedy and later held a position on the Cincinnati City Council in 1971. (He resigned in 1974, after the news broke that he'd used a personal check to solicit a prostitute, but then ran for the office again in 1975 and won by a landslide.) But the show had abysmal ratings and, in 1993, was overhauled to be less about politics and more about sleazy, tabloidesque topics like cheating scandals, porn addictions, or people hiding their queer lives from their significant others.

And then there's the fighting. When infidelity or other secrets were revealed on the show, in episodes like "You Slept with My Stripper Sister!" and "I'm Proud to Be a Homewrecker," the studio audience was often witness to slap fights and closed-fist brawls. Security would break up the melee, but only after every participant got a few licks in and the audience could erupt into chants of "Jerry! Jerry! Jerry!" to egg the fighters on. Now, given my gran's harsh rules for TV consumption, do you think I was allowed to watch *Jerry Springer*? Of course I was. The adult content felt even more cartoonish than the actual cartoon antics of Bart Simpson.

In an interview with CNN in 1998, ahead of his memoir's release, Springer said, "The truth is these are everyday people. They are everyday people caught in an outrageous situation, but they are our neighbors. They live in our neighborhoods, and sometimes they are us; they're in our own families." In the same interview, however, he rightfully said he was doing a show about "outrageousness" and not normal behavior, and that's exactly why it felt like fiction.

The guests on *Jerry Springer* were not *our* people. The majority of them were white (*Maury*, for better or stereotypical worse with its constant "who's the daddy" episodes, *seemed* more Black than *Jerry Springer*), and to quote Aviva Drescher on *The Real Housewives of New York* dressing down castmates Ramona Singer and Sonja Morgan, they were "white trash, quite frankly."

A lot of Black millennials grew up to learn that despite their families contributing to Democrat voting blocs, the values we were raised with were highly conservative, whether it be through a religious upbringing or the literal definition of the word, which means to be "averse to change or innovation and holding traditional values." My family, who made roots in Milwaukee after an upbringing in Tennessee, were part of the Black migration that created white flight, a departure of middle-class white people from areas that were becoming more ethnically diverse. Though I didn't attend an all-white school until high school, I often had white friends growing up because my family remained devoted to "movin' on up" like *The Jeffersons.** We tended to move frequently to "better neighborhoods," which usually meant predominantly white ones.

When I visit home, our neighborhood is now full of other Black families, but I distinctly remember when we were the first ones on the block, so the white people on *Jerry Springer* seemed like made-up caricatures of white people. When Black people *did* appear on the show, just like how a light-skinned Black businesswoman in a Tyler Perry movie looks down on a dark-skinned Black man with a service-industry job, we acknowledged those weren't *our* kind of Black people. They didn't have our economic status, and we certainly didn't have deadbeat dads or incarcer-

---

* *The Jeffersons* was a 1975 spin-off of Norman Lear's *All in the Family*, starring Sherman Hemsley and Isabel Sanford as George and Louise Jefferson, a Black family who was able to "move on up" to the Upper East Side of Manhattan due to their successful chain of dry-cleaning businesses.

ated people in our families. Except, we did have both of those problems and more (LOL at the gall to act bougie when we were also buying groceries with food stamps* in the early nineties). Still, in a conservative family, whether it's white or Black, you whisper about those problems when you think the kids aren't listening, and then you cosplay Black excellence in public.

My other fascination with *Jerry Springer* was that it had the queerest representation on TV I'd ever seen—transsexuals, bisexuals, secret gay affairs, prostitutes. I can be real here: Clearly, Springer didn't set out to create a pro-queer TV series, but the series was the diametric opposite of the "family values" that George H. W. Bush had declared he would usher a return to only a few years earlier. Even in the non-queer episodes, the show was a rejection of heteronormativity that I found just as titillating as the soft-core porn I'd been sneak-watching on cable in the middle of the night. But *Jerry Springer* I could safely watch in the middle of the afternoon with my family.

I had a gay uncle, Bill, who lived with his partner, Kevin, but they resided in Chicago and by the time I grew into my adolescence and started to realize that I was gay, my uncle was dead. The mere knowledge that I'd had a gay uncle who we visited often and who my family loved deeply was never quite enough to give me a voice to say that I *myself* was gay, and I didn't even know what that meant anyway, apart from the things I watched on TV. And while the people on *Jerry Springer* "weren't us," they *felt* like me, or at least I found a great thrill in watching someone with a swishy walk and lisp challenge a conservative housewife on national TV and tell her, "Bitch, I'm sleeping with your man!"

---

* Well, *I* was buying groceries, because it was less embarrassing for Mom to send me to the grocery store with food stamps.

It was refreshing seeing vulgar, overtly sexual, and dramatic queer people on TV flaunting their sexuality and sex-work careers without any shame, and to see them celebrated for that among my family and my peers, who couldn't wait to talk about the latest *Jerry Springer* episode when we got to school the next day. It was particularly refreshing since I grew up in Milwaukee in the nineties, and if you know anything about that period,* then you know that serial killer and cannibal Jeffrey Dahmer murdered a lot of queer people of color and kept their body parts in his apartment—the ones that he didn't eat, that is.

The nineties had several highly televised scandals—the Bill Clinton and Monica Lewinsky affair, O. J. Simpson's murder trial, Anita Hill's Senate testimony—but the one that is forever seared into my brain began July 23, 1991, when the nightly news revealed that Dahmer had been arrested at his home in the Oxford Apartments on 924 North 25th Street, which was not far from where we lived or from the Montessori school I attended at the time. I was barely old enough to register any of this news, but the myth of Dahmer as a boogeyman continued to haunt Milwaukee at least throughout my childhood, and I certainly knew from a cousin of mine that he killed "Black faggots," so it was no surprise that some of my most vivid nightmares as a child involved Jeffrey Dahmer skinning me alive. Inexplicably, in the nightmares, he was dressed like Santa Claus, because perhaps the idea of someone sneaking into our home even to drop off presents and scarf down milk and cookies was terrifying to me.

The nightmares were also thanks to our frequent babysitter, Mom's friend Lisa, whose method of babysitting was let-

---

* Or watched that Ryan Murphy Netflix series that I will never watch, but I'm glad it finally got Niecy Nash her Primetime Emmy.

ting us watch the Nightmare on Elm Street films while she listened to R&B albums in her bedroom. Most of the time, it was Toni Braxton's debut album on repeat, so whenever I heard the song "Breathe Again," I had flashbacks to Freddy Krueger making a teenage boy into a marionette with his veins. For years, you couldn't tell me "Breathe Again" wasn't in the closing credits to *Dream Warriors* until I purchased the DVD box set in high school and learned it was not, in fact, on any of the Nightmare on Elm Street soundtracks. But that didn't stop the song from accompanying the cannibal Santa Claus who tried to murder me in my nightmares well into adulthood.

I knew Dahmer's victims were all male, and I knew they were mostly young men of color, and news reports always managed to mention that Dahmer fucked the corpses he kept too, which would be described as "gay shit" on my school playground and scared me out of any probability that I myself would identify as gay.

Maybe it was better not to have a rebel like Bart Simpson as an early role model. Boys who didn't do what they were told, like "don't be gay," could end up dead. After all, the only gay people I knew of were dead. Like my uncle. And those boys in that nearby apartment building.

These bitches overall is some Lauras, they Winslow.

—AZEALIA BANKS, "ANNA WINTOUR" (2018)

• • • • •

BEING STEVE URKEL

I don't think about my father. Consciously, I know this to be true. Subconsciously, I know it's a lie because I have vivid memories of a classmate at New York University asking why everything I wrote was about my relationship with him. I avoided therapy for years after that. Because she was right. I'd managed to finally reach my dream school, that "glorified state school," according to *Gossip Girl*'s Blair Waldorf, and I got to wander Greenwich Village scribbling ideas for scripts in my notepad at late-night diner Cozy Soup 'n' Burger* like a mix between Spike Lee and Carrie Bradshaw while also slinging cupcakes for below minimum wage at Magnolia Bakery. Most of my time at NYU's Tisch School of the Arts involved me writing plays and screenplays that were my brain's attempt to work out my lingering daddy issues.

I do think about him, I suppose, since it'd be impossible not to do as a writer who crafts fictional stories. I mine my family dynamics for inspiration like most of my gay forefathers of dramatic writing: Tennessee Williams, James Baldwin,[†] and Tony

---

* Which closes at ten p.m. now, which is bullshit, even though it is overpriced and annoying. But that's most places frequented by NYU students.

† In addition to his essays and some of the most devastating books you'll ever read, James Baldwin wrote two plays: *The Amen Corner* (1954) and *Blues for Mister Charlie* (1964).

Kushner, to name a few. So, let's talk about Andre, a man I have maybe three actual vivid memories of. I spent much of my childhood being *told* what Andre was like by various people who really ought to have known better. On the occasion when he is discussed, it's rarely in front of me. My family is very good at burying topics, like the Fisher family from *Six Feet Under*, but our funeral home is metaphorical, and all the bodies are familial strife. My most distinct memory of Andre is arriving at a family gathering (his side) on the other end of town. His family had frequent cookouts that included mac and cheese that wasn't made how Gran made it, so I never ate it, and me sweating through my shirt after being shooed from outside with whatever book I was reading to be forced into interacting with cousins whose names I couldn't even remember and only saw once a year.

I was usually taken by my paternal grandfather, Henry, who we all refer to as Papaw. He has stayed in my life despite Andre's absence. Upon arrival, I'd be told earnestly by multiple aunts and uncles, "Your dad and brother were just here!" Half brother, for the record. I have a half brother I've met maybe once in my life. The performance the relatives on my dad's side put on every time I saw them, as if they didn't know I'd had no relationship with Andre since my sister was born, was insulting enough to make me never form a relationship with any of them. And at this point, who knows if there are more half siblings I've never even heard of? Showing up at extended-family events hoping to run into Andre was a lot like waiting for service at Soho House. It's not happening anytime soon, but good luck!

My graduate school writing class was a lightbulb moment for me: I realized that your relationship with your parents *does* influence your art—not just the art you create, but the art you consume and how you interpret it. Thanks to films like *Bambi* and *Finding Nemo*, we know that people with mommy issues have an unhealthy obsession with Disney.

Our own paternal and maternal issues are never more evidenced than through the types of sitcoms we enjoy. For example, 1950s Hollywood was very insistent on upholding white patriarchal values: that's why we had the Cleavers on *Leave It to Beaver* and the Andersons on *Father Knows Best*—a presumptuous title that surely has proven to be an oxymoron at this point. Stay-at-home wives like June Cleaver and husbands like Ward Cleaver who were hardworking and stern but ultimately loving in the final scene of each episode. Theodore Cleaver, nicknamed Beaver, would usually get into some kind of trouble that he'd hide from his parents. June would find out about it and try to problem-solve before Ward found out. Unsurprisingly, Ward always found out, and then he'd give Beaver a life lesson at the end of the episode, and the Cleavers would chuckle hearty Caucasians laughs[*] as the credits rolled.

Over time, audiences grew to want to watch maternal figures on TV rather than paternal ones. The "father knows best" mantra had gone out of vogue since working dads rarely knew what the hell was going on in their homes during the day, and advertisers realized that women might want to see *other* women on TV solving problems like they had to in their everyday lives. But soon, the moms on TV became the ones actually watching people's kids.

The term "latchkey kid" was used to describe Gen X kids and elder millennials who were left at home to fend for themselves during their formative years. These were kids whose par-

---

[*] You know, a tilted-back head, a deep-throated guffaw, and something like the word "sport" uttered.

ents were at work when they got home from school or who were left at home during the day with no adult supervision. It cracks me up whenever parents today are worried about how much time their kids spend looking at screens, because from middle school to high school, millennials woke up and watched syndicated TV in the morning: usually cartoons on Disney, *Charmed*, or *Saved by the Bell* and *USA High*, a two-season show that aired on USA Network about American kids in a Parisian boarding school that inexplicably has ninety-five episodes. It made no one famous and I've never seen any of the leads ever again. If you told the average millennial this show never existed, they'd probably believe you or likely mistake it for the one-season Ryan Gosling sitcom *Breaker High,* about a high school on a cruise ship.

Most teachers started figuring out how to stick their students in front of computers to avoid interacting with them during the manifest destiny era of the internet, which involved us learning HTML, playing *Number Munchers* and *The Oregon Trail*, and spending copious amounts of time crafting the perfect AIM away message. AOL Instant Messenger was the de facto chat room for all high school students. When you were unavailable to chat, you would write a usually clever message about what you were doing instead of sitting in front of a computer, or you'd just put Fall Out Boy or My Chemical Romance lyrics as a subtle hint at a crush you had or a friend you were upset with.

After school, millennials were once again glued to their TV sets until dinner and then again after dinner and then once more after they were sure their parents were asleep. This is how we watched the sexy MTV soap opera *Undressed* that aired after ten p.m. and included storylines involving threesomes and an introduction to the fact that college apparently meant spending a lot of time in the laundry room, not just for laundry, but also for sex.

Basically, we watched a lot of TV. None more than kids born between 1980 and 1984, who are either younger Gen X or elder millennial, depending on who you ask. They were raised on new television and reruns of their parents' shows on Nick at Nite, which is why that generation is the most knowledgeable about pop culture that precedes them. You can call them Generation Catalano, after Jared Leto's heartthrob character Jordan Catalano on *My So-Called Life*, a one-season series starring Claire Danes that is very important to anyone who caught it when it aired in 1994 and is mostly an anecdote to anyone born after 1985.

But back to sitcoms. Not to be a BuzzFeed personality quiz, but the sitcoms you watched in your formative years tended to mirror the family unit you *wished* you had. For many American families that didn't represent the nuclear family, sitcoms were aspirational. Families stuck together no matter what—except for characters written off shows like they never existed (but we'll get to that when I talk about *Family Matters*)—and always hugged it out at the end of the episode, and never minded the validating cheers and laughter from the studio audience. For Black millennials, there are three sitcoms that tap into our unfulfilled desires or, as I will call it, wish fulfillment for an idealized family unit, wealth and privilege, and generally being regarded as "cool."*

There's the show we all love because it's a good show: *The*

---

* Most modern comedies suffer from the idea that *all* characters should be "cool" and "relatable," a disease largely created by *Friends*, not because of the characters but because of the actors, despite the existence of David Schwimmer, who has never been remotely cool.

Fresh Prince of Bel-Air. There's the show that we all love despite it being bad: *The Cosby Show.* And then there's the show that has not been fondly remembered at all and has drawn the frequent ire of millennials whenever they want to go viral online with a hot take, but it's actually great: *Family Matters.*

I'll explain.

The Fresh Prince of Bel-Air is an indisputably excellent show. If you hate it, find some taste. Debuting in 1990, it was a bridge from a decade of *Lifestyles of the Rich and Famous* culture to the implosion of late-eighties and early-nineties hip-hop culture. It was for everyone who watched *Dynasty* and secretly wished the real star was Diahann Carroll's Dominique Deveraux. *Dynasty* was primarily a soap about rich white people until Carroll joined as, in her own words, "the first Black bitch on TV." She first appeared chastising a hotel employee for not providing her with a larger suite, which immediately let you know that she wasn't just the first Black bitch on TV; she was a bougie bitch too. Dominique spent most of her time on the series swilling champagne and trading barbs with Joan Collins's Alexis Colby.

Like the invention of Dominique, *Fresh Prince* was Black-excellence bait. Philip Banks was the stern, lovable father we'd seen countless variations of on TV before—but this one was Black. And wealthy, not because of a job in entertainment or because his blue-collar business blew up like George and Weezy's,* but because he was a prominent, well-respected judge. *The Jeffersons* represented the so-called American dream that we're all constantly striving for, but *Fresh Prince* existed in a world where Black people were able to thrive as equally as their white peers. Or so it would seem. Many of the best *Fresh Prince*

---

* A nickname for Louise Jefferson, referenced also in Will Smith's 1997 single "Gettin' Jiggy wit It."

episodes reminded the characters that no matter how much wealth they accumulated, they were still Black and would be treated as such, like when Will and his cousin Carlton are pulled over by the police for driving a nice car.

Philip's wife, Vivian Banks, was the dignified, regal (and rich, don't forget that) mom many viewers wished they had. Hilary Banks was the rich-bitch daughter who everyone secretly wished they were, even if they told themselves they'd never be as obnoxious as she was, but you probably would be just as obnoxious if you were gorgeous, light-skinned, and born into a wealthy Black family in Los Angeles. I would be! Hilary became such an aspirational icon for a lot of Black girls that referring to them as a Hilary Banks was shorthand for calling them uppity and white-acting. The same insult could be lobbed at boys by referring to them as a Carlton Banks.

Carlton was the annoying brother who acted as a representation of viewers' own irritating siblings. He also dressed like a yuppie and spoke in an affected (white) manner and looked down on people with less privilege than him, which often caused him to clash with his cousin Will and other Black characters on the series. He was one of the first television personifications of Black excellence as a negative and a means to achieve white approval. In contrast to Hilary and Carlton, their cool younger sister, Ashley, was the first to befriend their cousin Will from Philadelphia. She was more in tune with Black youth culture. Ashley dressed like a regular Black teenager in the nineties rather than someone trying to fit in on *Beverly Hills, 90210*. Though she also existed in a world of privilege, she rebelled against it more than her siblings did.

Then there's Geoffrey, the family's butler. It is fair to say the majority of *Fresh Prince*'s viewing audience didn't have a butler at home, which is why his role's purpose on the series was dual—to show how rich the Banks family was, but also to mock them for how privileged they were. If the Bankses were going to be a relatable family, you needed a regular cast member to knock them down a few pegs in each scene. Those old enough to remember Robert Guillaume as butler Benson in the eponymous sitcom *Benson* (or the superior series it was spun off from, *Soap*) were glad that Geoffrey didn't have to do his stand-up routine for a white family.

This is the entire model for the success of *The O.C.*, by the way. Which is why once wrong-side-of-the-tracks Ryan Atwood is fully integrated into the Cohen family and starts behaving like every other rich kid on the show, the entire concept fell apart and the ratings dropped.

And then there was the series' protagonist, Will, played by Will Smith. Smith, then part of the rap duo DJ Jazzy Jeff & the Fresh Prince, would go on to become an even more famous rapper and movie star beloved by Black and white people alike . . . until he slapped Chris Rock during the 2022 Oscars telecast. If you're reading this in a distant future where the Slap is not something you can immediately recall, first, congrats to me for someone reading this book long after I'm dead. Second, I hope that since then everyone has regained their collective minds and gotten over the outrage that ensued when Smith slapped Rock for a *G.I. Jane* joke about Smith's wife Jada Pinkett Smith's bald head.

The thing about the joke is that it was bad, because *G.I. Jane* is an unimportant 1997 film starring Demi Moore as the first woman to take part in special ops military training. The film failed at the box office, because it's very bad, but Moore famously shaved her head for the role and called it her proudest professional achievement in her 2019 memoir *Inside Out*—an exceptionally good celebrity memoir, so I'll forgive her.

I think Smith was as offended by the lazy joke as he was by the insult against his wife. I contend that the slap would have never occurred if the reference were something like Charlize Theron's character Furiosa in *Mad Max: Fury Road*. Then we could've avoided the endless debate over whether Rock deserved the slap, or if Smith's actions were grossly violent (girl, it was a slap), or if white actors would ever feel *safe* attending the Oscars again. But we were not spared any of those talking points for what seemed like an eternity (it was a full year, for the record) because of a goddamn *G.I. Jane* reference, a weak insult exhausted by teenage boys on elementary school playgrounds in the nineties. *G.I. Jane* has never been brought up in the context of its merits as a film; rather it's mostly been used as a punch line against bald or otherwise-masculine-presenting girls and women.

It's an insult I used to live in fear of, since Gran was a sergeant major in the army during most of my adolescence. I didn't see my gran as a badass who ran shit at army bases. I was embarrassed by them calling her G.I. Jane! That is, until one time she picked me up in her fatigues and became a go-to chaperone for school events and trips. Then the kids at school liked her more than me, and the G.I. Jane jokes stopped. It's a testament to how insults are passed through generations. "G.I. Jane" replaced "your mother wears combat boots," which could simultaneously denote that your mom is poor or she's a dyke, or both.

On *Fresh Prince*, the theme song introduced Will Smith as the audience's surrogate, an everyman who found himself transported to the kingdom of Bel-Air. If only we could all be plucked from our circumstances and sent to live in a mansion in Bel-Air, complete with a butler. After one fight in his hometown of Philadelphia, Will was shipped off to live with his rich family relatives ("I got in one little fight and my mom got scared. And said, you're movin' with your auntie and uncle in Bel-Air").

There was an unnecessary 2022 reboot of the series titled *Bel-Air*, which reimagined the series as dark and gritty. It seemed its creator, Morgan Cooper (who initially made a gritty, pretty fantastic short-film take on the series), intended to add emotional depth to the series—an exploration of gang violence and being Black in white spaces, for instance. But that depth already existed in the original series, and the reboot only served to make the subtext of the series the text. Any Black viewer of *Fresh Prince* was astutely aware of what it was like to be Black in America in the nineties. Therefore, the series operated not only as a "what if?" to viewers who could imagine themselves living bougie in Bel-Air, but also had a built-in commentary on Blackness and the youth culture of the nineties.

An exploration of racism is central to the show, such as in the aforementioned episode where Carlton gets pulled over by the police. The show hints at our responsibility to learn our own history in episodes like the one where Will is doing worse in his African American studies class than the white students. Firing the series' first Aunt Viv, dark-skinned actress Janet Hubert, and replacing her with light-skinned Daphne Maxwell Reid explored colorism. I'm kidding. All right, maybe only a bit. The endless jokes that casting decision has sparked to this day on social media operate as an introduction to understanding colorism.

But the episode that most resonates with me, and perhaps with many *Fresh Prince* viewers, is when Ben Vereen appears in season four of the series as Will's deadbeat father, Lou. The scene seems to always be brought up when mentioning how "real" the series gets ("real," as in a dramatic episode that you took seriously, as opposed to a "very special episode" that no one, not even the people writing it, could have ever taken seriously). The appearance of Lou is mostly to service Will's relationship with Uncle Phil. Lou upset Phil from the jump, and Will's quick attachment to his biological father causes him to lash out at his surrogate father. "I'm sorry everyone can't be as perfect as you," Will says to his uncle Phil, admonishing him for not even being willing to give Lou a second chance after he apologizes for abandoning his family. Will plans to leave his home in Bel-Air and go on the road with his dad, telling Phil point-blank: "You are not my father!" But as expected, Will's biological dad essentially ghosts him. There's no real explanation for it other than Lou is a terrible father.

Nor is there motive for his sudden appearance in Will's life. Is it guilt? Or is that just a motive Will and the audience create in their minds, the same way I come up with my own motives for why my dad stopped being in my family's lives? There's a very emotional moment where Will cries and asks his uncle Phil, "How come he don't want me, man?" and it's one of my favorite scenes of TV, if only because a Black male gets an opportunity to be completely vulnerable with another Black male, which was practically unheard of on TV in the nineties and is still pretty much an anomaly today.*

Fresh Prince holds up incredibly well on rewatch not only because it's funny, but because it taps into the desire most Americans have for a strong family. Granted, it's been instilled in us by the patriarchy or whatever, but when you watch the

---

* Except in the Best Man franchise, which is all about sad and depressed Black men who can only be saved by the (probably) platonic love of another man— the audience for that franchise is non-heterosexual men, so I fear few lessons have been learned from it.

Banks family on TV, you wish they were *your* parents, not just because they live in a mansion, but because there's a sense of a mother and a father with a strong moral compass. Things I didn't have, things I didn't know I craved. Or maybe I just really wished my ass were that rich.

The same, obviously, can be said about *The Cosby Show*. Cliff and Clair Huxtable were the model image of Black upward mobility when the series debuted in 1984. With a dearth of positive images of Black people, let alone Black families, on TV, the Huxtables operated as a new Black American dream. Cliff is a well-respected ob-gyn with his own practice. Clair is a lawyer without an *E* in her name because she's not like you regular bitches, okay?* The Huxtables began the series with four children. Denise, the free-spirited bougie-boho daughter with a mix of hairstyles from locs to tomboy cuts, portrayed by Lisa Bonet,† eventually becomes the show's most popular character due to Bonet's screen presence and budding celebrity.

There's Theo, the perennial-screwup son who usually learns a lesson at the end of episodes centering him. And by the way, Malcolm-Jamal Warner is very funny, and the role he *should* be remembered for more is from the 1996 UPN series *Malcolm & Eddie*, a show watched regularly by about three million viewers during its four-year tenure, which would be a certified hit by today's Nielsen ratings standards, but to put things in perspective, the number one show of 1996 was *ER*, with an average of 21.2 million viewers.

Now, back to the Cosbys: Vanessa and Rudy are their other daughters, and I frankly don't remember a single thing either

---

* I mean, she is bilingual! She has a perfect streak on Duolingo.

† "Free-spirited" is an understatement. In the nineties, she changed her name to Lilakoi Moon while still being credited professionally as Lisa Bonet.

of them did on the show, but they were very cute! Midway through the first season, a fifth child was introduced: eldest daughter Sondra, who was off at Princeton and signifies the overall problem with *The Cosby Show*. Sondra was introduced because Bill Cosby allegedly wanted to show the Huxtables successfully raising a child who was a college graduate. The reason I hate *The Cosby Show* is that very few creative decisions on the show were made because they were *entertaining* choices. They were made because they were choices that made the Huxtables look like a Good Black Family. I have never had a conversation with anyone who remembers *The Cosby Show* fondly as an entertaining show. Being like the Huxtables has become synonymous with having your shit together, sure, but the show wasn't particularly funny.

And most of the Theo storylines revolved around his father's disdain for him. And every Denise story you remember as entertaining was stolen from *A Different World*, a far superior TV show. Any show that introduces us to Whitley Gilbert and Dwayne Wayne is already getting put in the TV sitcom canon, but to this day, the 1992 episode where Dwayne interrupts Whitley's wedding to Byron Douglas is still one of the most iconic episodes of TV ever. There's no singular episode of *The Cosby Show* that would make any list of iconic TV episodes. Most people remember *The Cosby Show* for the way it made them feel—at its most innocuous, it was another type of wish-fulfillment series like *Fresh Prince*.

It gave Black viewers an aspirational but mostly *respectable* version of themselves on TV each week. Which is understandable—there weren't other Black people on TV at the time! But it feels a lot like the kind of show people still wish we had on TV. When people decry multifaceted Black stories and call them "trauma porn" or insist we only have slave movies in theaters, what they really just want are stories about bougie, upwardly mobile Black folks they can aspire to be.

At its worst, *The Cosby Show* gave white people the impression that racism was over and that if Black people wanted better lives, well, then, they should just be like the Huxtables. I don't particularly care what white people think about *The Cosby Show*, because the only ones with strong opinions about the series four decades later are probably Republicans, rich comedy writers, or dead. What Black people think of *The Cosby Show*, however, is something that I care about a lot.

The show is often brought up in comparison to *Family Matters*, which—let's get it out of the way—has some of the most absurd writing I have ever seen on a TV series. If you happened to tune in to the series premiere on September 22, 1989, and then only checked back in for the series finale on July 17, 1998, your head would spin at the fact that a series about a working-class Black family in Chicago was now centered around Steve Urkel (who you've never met before, seeing as how he was introduced in the series' twelfth episode as a minor character). We used to have an abundance of working-class Black shows, from *227* to *Roc*, but the push for "more diverse" stories on TV has mostly meant we don't see realistic portrayals of Black people on-screen across America; we just see sanitized versions that won't get executives in trouble.

The last season of *Family Matters* centers on Steve Urkel's engagement to the Winslow family's eldest daughter, Laura—sorry, *only* daughter, because the youngest sibling, Judy, was written out of the series in 1993 and never mentioned again—and his attempts to return home to her *from space*, where he was currently lost. Ironically, the series abandoning its working-class roots is what earns it so much derision today, but there are very few "working-class" Black sitcoms that have succeeded beyond the heyday of 227. The late-eighties introduction of the Huxtables can be seen as a direct line from "good representation" of Black people on TV to only bougie, well-off Black people being depicted on TV, outside of crime dramas.

Family Matters was over-the-top, and yes, Steve Urkel's campy, borderline-sci-fi and, eventually, literal-sci-fi storylines— Stefan Urquelle? I'll get to him in a minute—and his catchphrase, "Did I do that?" did threaten to take over the series. But with as much retroactive hate as the series gets, you'd wonder why the ratings didn't flatline before the series was moved from ABC to CBS. And that's because people didn't particularly *mind* the outlandish storylines. Black families' TV habits in the nineties included a healthy dose of sitcoms, cop shows, and soap operas, and Steve Urkel building a machine that turns him into a cool version of himself named Stefan Urquelle and then later cloning a version of himself to make Stefan a permanent character is hardly mind-bending to audiences who've seen two Krystle Carringtons on *Dynasty*, Marlena Evans possessed by the devil on *Days of Our Lives*, and Sheila Carter stealing babies and surviving death every other year on *The Young and the Restless*.

There's a tendency in critiques of comedy to claim something isn't funny if it's not the type of comedy you're into. Slapstick and camp aren't genres that everyone loves, and they're not particularly in vogue right now. Most TV comedies don't even have jokes in them (which would be an opportunity for a certain show about a British football team to catch some strays from me if I didn't find that show and Jason Sudeikis incredibly charming), which is why network executives are surely baffled by the success of *Abbott Elementary*, a show that thrives on actual jokes. Most comedies on TV aren't really funny like classic sitcoms were anymore. TV these days is full of lightly comic situations or dramas masquerading as comedies, because jokes require actual, defined characters, and defined characters are polarizing, much like real human beings. Having rewatched every single episode of *Family Matters* for the purpose of writing this book, I can safely say that the show is really fucking funny.

Aside from the claim that the show was never funny, there are two major critiques that *Family Matters* receives that are *mostly* valid. One: Steve Urkel is a stalker. He basically harasses Laura into falling in love with him. I'm not here to argue that he's *not* giving *Fatal Attraction*, but I will also posit that the majority of male TV and film characters in the eighties and nineties were male fantasies of how love worked. If you just wait long enough, they'll eventually fall in love with you. Think of Screech on *Saved by the Bell*. Think of John Cusack in *Say Anything*. Eventually, Laura is written as actually having feels for Urkel, but Steve's penance is her wanting a hotter and cooler version of him (Stefan) while she treats him like garbage. Also, we are introduced to a character named Myra, who's just as insanely obsessed with Steve as he is with Laura. I once again return to the fact that audiences familiar with soap operas are not unfamiliar with characters' motivations being changed on a writer's whim. One of the best series of the nineties, *Melrose Place*—a series that started as depicting sexy young adults living in a West Hollywood apartment building that eventually turned into stories like Dr. Kimberly Shaw coming back from the dead and blowing up the apartment complex—was literally built around characters changing their motivations every other week at the whims of the writers. *Family Matters* should be allowed to do the same thing.

The second most common critique is that the series centers around the fact that Carl Winslow, the family patriarch, is a cop.

In Chicago. He's literally the opps. Black people have a long history of playing law enforcement in TV and films, which is in a sense propaganda to make Black people more comfortable with police and also a way for Black characters to have "respectable" jobs. Carl being a cop is no more conservative of an ideal than the entirety of *The Cosby Show*, so who cares? I would put a wager on there not being a single Black person who has watched *Family Matters* and wanted to become a cop because *Carl Winslow* was a fucking cop. He's a *Simpsons* parody of a cop mixed with a bit of Homer Simpson himself: a bumbling father figure who is far from an advertisement for the boys in blue. I bet you'd find a ton of Black people who became cops because of Eddie Murphy in the Beverly Hills Cop movies and Danny Glover in *Lethal Weapon*, however.

I do have the tendency to give leeway to things that make me cry. Keep in mind, I've cried at *WALL·E*, so take this opinion with a grain of salt, but the trauma beneath Urkel's character is that his family essentially abandons him and leaves the Winslows to put up with him. And throughout the show, he develops a father-son relationship and genuine friendship with Carl. When I think of sitcoms that made me sincerely wish for a relationship with Andre, I don't think of *The Cosby Show*—my family was never gonna be the Huxtables, and most of the time Cliff didn't even seem to like Theo.

I loved Will's relationship with his uncle Phil in *Fresh Prince*, but who *wouldn't* want someone cool enough to literally be referred to as the "fresh prince" to be their son? But Steve Urkel, who was kinda weird and a nerd and who didn't fit in with anyone else, finding a father figure who, deep down, actually loved him? At a certain point in the series, Urkel's absentee parents abandon him further by leaving the country, and Carl becomes his de facto father. If anything, *Family Matters* then becomes a buddy series starring Urkel and Carl—a lost kid and his father figure getting into the bizarrest of situations, like wrestling matches and cloning mishaps.

Carl accidentally electrocutes himself in an episode and nearly dies, and the series suddenly becomes a dramatic *Grey's Anatomy* scene as Urkel performs CPR on him and brings him back to life just to drive home how much they love each other. I constantly think about that. Which I guess means that sometimes, I am constantly thinking about my father.

Oh my goodness!

—MARTIN LAWRENCE AS SHENENEH, *MARTIN* (1992–1997)

. . . . .

DAMN, GINA!

Picture this: I'm an investigative reporter going undercover at a local high school to accomplish the one thing I never did in high school. My unfulfilled moment, like Drew Barrymore achieving her first high school kiss in *Never Been Kissed*, would be getting cast in a school play. *Any* of them.

For my entire high school tenure, I was never even given a minor part in a single school production, except for a production of *Hello, Dolly!* put on by our all-girls sister school, Divine Savior Holy Angels. Millennials who read young adult trash before the Gossip Girl and Pretty Little Liars book series made it cool might be familiar with the 2005 novel *Whores on the Hill*, a Bret Easton Ellis–esque take on DSHA in the eighties, written by former student Colleen Curran. The book caused a minor uproar among our recently graduated class, but not enough to become national news and spur a film adaptation starring Hilary Duff or something. I'm not saying I was giving Denzel Washington[*] in those high school theater auditions, but I wasn't giving John David Washington[†] either.

I don't particularly blame our frequent directors Ms. Halston and Father Wilkinson for not casting me in anything. I probably

---

[*] The greatest living actor!

[†] Son of the greatest living actor!

sucked. To this day, I still need a shot of vodka and an amphetamine to feel comfortable onstage. Call it stage fright, but there's still something about standing on a stage and presenting myself to a group of strangers that makes my skin slightly crawl. Which probably sounds odd for someone who's developed a career that usually involves performing and for someone who enjoys the attributes of their astrological sign Leo, but I didn't always have a fear of performing. When I was younger, I loved attention. Before I learned how to center myself in my writing like a young Carrie Bradshaw, recess was my favorite part of school. During the height of *Mighty Morphin Power Rangers*, I loved to play Power Rangers with my classmates. This involved everyone taking on a Power Ranger and reenacting fight scenes from the show. I was usually the Pink Ranger, which annoyed the girls.

Power Rangers first aired on American TV in the summer of 1993 as part of Fox Kids, a children's programming block that debuted in 1990 with the series *Attack of the Killer Tomatoes* (a weird animated series based on the parody horror franchise of the same name, which has produced only one funny film, its first sequel, *Return of the Killer Tomatoes*, which I rented from a video store once because George Clooney is in it) and *Bobby's World*, an incredibly cute animated series voiced by Howie Mandel from when he was a comedian[*] and not the host of *America's Got Talent*, which has somehow been on air longer than the Confederacy existed. I question how good Mandel is at

---

[*] Millennials mostly have no concept of who Howie Mandel is, except for knowing he was on TV a lot and sometimes they mistakenly believe he was in RadioShack commercials with Teri Hatcher (that was Howie *Long*). People older than millennial age will remember him from *St. Elsewhere*. And most people of any age tend to be shocked when you tell them Mandel voiced Gizmo in the Gremlins franchise (of which the sequel, *Gremlins 2: The New Batch*, is woefully missing from the Criterion Collection).

this job as a detective of talent if it's taken him this long to find any. Two years after *Power Rangers, Batman: The Animated Series* and *X-Men* debuted on Fox Kids, and it became appointment TV for me after school.

So, when *Mighty Morphin Power Rangers* debuted, I was hooked from the first episode. The series initially revolved around five teenagers in the fictional California city of Angel Grove—Jason the Red Ranger, Trini the Yellow Ranger, Zack the Black Ranger, Kimberly the Pink Ranger, and Billy the Blue Ranger—who saved the world from alien monsters. They were given their powers by Zordon, who used to be a human but was now a floating head in a tube. Weird sci-fi shit you just went with as a kid. Zordon's assistant, Alpha 5, was a gay robot.

For some reason, no one in the town of Angel Grove knew that these teenagers were the five Power Rangers who saved them from aliens each week. The Power Rangers always wore the colors of their respective identities. The Pink Ranger always wore pink clothing, even out of uniform. The Red Ranger always wore red clothing. The Blue Ranger always wore blue, and so on. This mildly terrified me for their safety as a kid, because kids in the nineties in Milwaukee heavily believed the urban legend that wearing anything red or blue would get you mistaken for a Blood or a Crip and shot in a drive-by. The Power Rangers also frequently used their watches and walkie-talkies in a pre–Apple Watch era.

Not noticing Clark Kent is Superman is one thing—have you ever seen a friend who always wears contacts suddenly appear with glasses? I couldn't identify them in a police lineup. But it should have been very easy to figure out the Power Rangers' secret identities!

Power Rangers was a surprisingly gay series, and not just because of the gay robot, Alpha 5. Lord Zedd, one of the series'

most prominent villains, was a real-life Tom of Finland draw-
ing with no skin on his body, so you could see his ripped, red
muscles and veins underneath silver metallic body armor. Ivan
Ooze, first introduced in the 1995 film *Mighty Morphin Power
Rangers: The Movie*, literally swanned about in a cape like Tru-
man Capote (he sounded the same, too). Then there was
Tommy Oliver, my true *Power Rangers* gay awakening. He was
the Green Ranger when he was brainwashed by Rita to take
down the Power Rangers and then became the White Ranger
when he turned to the side of good. He had long stoner hair
and muscles constantly on display via ripped sleeveless shirts.
Not only was I into Tommy, but Mom was too. If she was
gonna have to watch *Power Rangers* with me every day, at least
there was Tommy.

It should also be said that *Power Rangers* is an awful TV series. While it became a pop-culture phenomenon in the nineties, primarily due to the cool monsters and fun fight scenes, it
was cobbled together using stock action footage from the
early-nineties Japanese TV series *Kyōryū Sentai Zyuranger*. And
in the tradition of saccharine nineties kids TV, each episode
ended with a morality lesson. The show was *Saved by the Bell*
with action scenes, but with none of the jokes (or, honestly, acting) that made *Saved by the Bell* watchable.

It also spawned a series of knockoffs that were actually fun-
nier and better scripted than *Power Rangers*, like *Big Bad Beetle-
borgs* (about three kids who make a wish to become their
favorite comic book heroes, which also unleashes the comic
books' villains into the real world) and *VR Troopers* (about
three kids into martial arts who discover that monsters actually live in virtual reality videos games), but they *also* used
Japanese stock footage that ran out quickly, so only two seasons of each of those series ever came to fruition. Rewatching

episodes of *Power Rangers* when they hit Netflix one summer truly stretched the limits of nostalgia to its breaking point. Some things are better left in the past. Similarly, I also grew out of playing Power Rangers with my friends and sought to perform something else that would entertain my classmates. Preferably a solo venture where I didn't have to argue with a girl that I should play the Pink Ranger and then end up playing the Black Ranger anyway.

Then I discovered *Martin*.

In 1992, the only comedians with successful sitcoms named after them were Roseanne Barr and Jerry Seinfeld. Before Roseanne became a Batman villain whose main power is being racist and spreading the type of conspiracy theories that come with a literacy of reading only Bazooka Joe comic strips, her sitcom *Roseanne* debuted in 1988 on ABC. The show, which portrayed working-class white people, who'd all but vanished from TV during the height of eighties rich-people soap operas, became a sensation in its second season and topped the Nielsen ratings. In 1989, NBC found their own comedian to put their faith in and debuted *Seinfeld*. The show wasn't particularly successful in its early seasons, but thanks to NBC's belief in it (unheard of in today's streaming era, where shows are canceled before they even air if they don't have enough buzz online), its audience grew, and it topped the Nielsen ratings in 1994.

Seinfeld has grown to become one of the most influential comedies on TV. Airing on NBC alongside *Friends*, the show was easy to think of as just another comedy about young white people talking about sex and relationships. But if the show feels quintessentially New York, despite being filmed in Los Angeles, it's because Seinfeld, with co-creator Larry David, managed to create a show that matched their Jewish East Coast sensibilities.

Seinfeld aired on Thursday nights alongside NBC's white,

upper-middle-class comedies. By the early nineties, Fox wanted to compete on Thursdays and began to invest in diverse programming like *In Living Color*, a sketch-comedy series created by Keenen Ivory Wayans; *Living Single*, a comedy about four single Black women in Brooklyn*; and *Martin*, a comedy starring comedian Martin Lawrence as a radio DJ in Detroit. Though *Martin* is remembered more for its sketch-comedy elements, like Lawrence playing several different characters in the show (he'd repeat this to great success in the successful but mostly unrewatchable Big Momma's House films†), it was also a subversive take on Black culture and the relationships between men and women. It shares much of its DNA with *Seinfeld* in that most of its jokes are culturally specific, it excels when it requires physical comedy from its stars, and it delivers a modern take on sexuality.

During the nineties, a show's time slot determined which audience it was for. If something aired at eight p.m., it was still considered a "family show." Somehow, once it became nine p.m., shows miraculously became for adults only. If something aired beyond ten p.m., all bets were off, and that's when women were raped and murdered on crime shows and you could see middle-aged-man ass on *NYPD Blue*. *Martin* aired at eight p.m., and so its overtly sexual jokes were seen as more "offensive" than the jokes on *In Living Color*, which aired at nine p.m., and even the jokes on the latter series often received pushback from Fox execs.

---

* *Living Single* is a hilarious comedy that will never develop its true legacy as an influential comedy until people learn to say anything else about it online besides, "*Friends* ripped it off."

† Lawrence's film oeuvre is full of bad comedies and the Bad Boys franchise (of which shockingly all films are great), but I wish more people remembered his most underrated film, *Blue Streak*.

Granted, some of the reactions to the humor on *Martin* were racist. In 1992, *Seinfeld* aired an episode titled "The Contest," where Jerry, George, Elaine, and Kramer make a bet to see who can last the longest without masturbating. NBC didn't like the term "masturbation" being used on prime-time TV, so the writers came up with the phrase "master of my domain" to describe someone who has resisted the urge to masturbate. The episode won an Emmy. In a 1993 *Martin* episode titled "Whoomp! There It Ain't," after Martin and his girlfriend, Gina, sneak out of her friend Pam's party to, well, get jiggy with it, Pam challenges them to abstain from sex for two weeks, which prompts them to make a bet to see who will be the first to give in. A December 15, 1993, review of the episode in the *Los Angeles Times* refers to the episode as "sex-crazy."

The review goes to great lengths to depict Lawrence in the most puritanical of terms: "When Gina wore a body-hugging, open-backed dress to a party, Martin's biological urges soared to 10 on the Richter scale. Bumping, grinding and pawing, he was all over her in public—his body pumping like a piston, his tongue thrusting lewdly—acting generally like an animal." Writer Howard Rosenberg (who begins his review lamenting the fact that he has to trash a series that won an NAACP award because it might make him seem racist) admonishes Fox for airing such an episode when it would be "available to young kids galore" and then goes on to absurdly relate the episode to Anita Hill's 1991 accusations of sexual harassment against then–U.S. Supreme Court nominee Clarence Thomas.

"Some African Americans were among those who loudly accused Hill then of evoking an ugly stereotype about black males being oversexed and definable by their sexual prowess and genitalia. Whether you agreed or disagreed with it being tied to Hill's testimony, the stereotype itself was no fantasy,

having roots in the centuries-old anti-black bias and igno-
rance from which much of this nation's history has evolved.
As Thomas himself said at the time, 'This plays into the most
bigoted, racist stereotypes that any black man will face.' A
stereotype nourished by *Martin*."

First, the gall to use that nigga Clarence Thomas to ad-
monish a TV sitcom is maybe the most retroactively hilarious
piece of pop-culture journalism outside of the *New York Times*
2003 headline "The Solo Beyoncé: She's No Ashanti."* Second,
there's a cruel irony in using the existence of harmful stereotypes of Black men *against* a Black man. It traffics in the type of
respectability politics that made *The Cosby Show* a success (naturally, Cosby even referred to Lawrence's hosting of HBO's *Def
Comedy Jam* as a "minstrel show") and invites Black people to
present sanitized versions of themselves not only for the consumption of white people, but also to gain the respect of other
Black people who are seeking white approval.

"You're not going to see us do anything that's coonish,"
Kenny Buford, a writer on *Martin*, told *Entertainment Weekly* in
1994. Buford, a former assistant to Spike Lee, joined the staff
after meeting Lawrence on the set of *Do the Right Thing*. Lawrence wanted the show to be over-the-top, and he wasn't interested in making white people comfortable. Unfortunately,
the series was canceled in its fifth season. And it remains that
the first four seasons of *Martin* were some of the funniest and
most inventive half hours of TV airing in the early nineties.
In the way *Seinfeld* inspired a generation of TV writers, *Martin*
did the same for Black comedy writers.

* Only in retrospect, mind you. Ashanti had *hits* in 2003, so this was a perfectly
reasonable headline at the time, even if it pitted two bad bitches against each
other for no reason beyond page views.

And for kids like me, thanks to one of Lawrence's most memorable roles on the series: Sheneneh Jenkins. Sheneneh, an exaggeration of a ghetto Black woman, was Martin's next-door neighbor who owned Sheneneh's Sho' Nuff Hair Salon. She was loud, wore flashy clothes, and hated Martin's girl-friend, Gina, and her friend Pam to the point that they almost came to blows each episode. Sheneneh became a breakout character in the way that Urkel became one on *Family Matters*, though people remember Sheneneh more fondly than they do Urkel, despite the obvious stereotypes she played into, but that's because *Martin* was made for Black audiences, not for white audiences to laugh at. And unlike Urkel, Sheneneh didn't eat up the show; she was merely part of a rotating repertoire of characters. Scenes with Sheneneh usually took place in the hallway between her and Martin's apartment and were five-ish-minute scenes where she spouted off one-liner insults at Martin's friends.

The first time I saw Sheneneh, I had no idea it was Lawrence. With the way he lived in the character, made her exaggerations seem human, made her comedy seem natural, she reminded me of my own mother when she got pissed off at a boyfriend or mad I told her "business" to teachers at school, or when she would light up a cigarette and listen to 2Pac and Biggie as she drove me to school most mornings. Whenever we watched *Martin* on Thursday nights (I wouldn't discover *Seinfeld* on Thursdays until *Martin*'s final two seasons, once Tisha Campbell left and it stopped being funny), Sheneneh got the most laughs. I instinctively picked up on this and began to imitate Sheneneh's mannerisms.

I first learned to imitate Lawrence's vocal inflections, then the physicality of the performance—the swishing of the hips, the bobblehead reactions. I began to replace playing Power Rangers with playing Sheneneh at school, at first during recess, but then one of the teachers at school noticed and found it funny. I don't even remember her name, but it was one of the first betrayals I'd ever experienced from an adult. She went from excitedly asking me to "do Sheneneh" at recess for her to calling my mother to complain the first time I "disrupted class" by doing her favorite impersonation.

I grew up in a household where whooping your kids ("a spanking," as white people call it) was commonplace. If you acted up at home or school, you could expect to be whooped later with a belt, or even worse, an elder relative might tell you, "Go get me a switch." A switch is a branch from a tree in the yard. It was even more terrifying because you had to go fetch the weapon yourself and hand it to them so they could whoop you with it. It was supposed to teach kids respect, I guess, but it mostly just made me cry and hate Mom, Gran, or anyone else until the anger left them hours later and I got a hug alongside a "you know I love you."

Many millennial-aged Black people have decided this is a tactic they never want to use to discipline their kids. I don't plan on having any, so it's a moot point, but I can't imagine personally doing that to even my niece on the days she pisses me off the most. I know the immediate flash of anger, the instinct to quickly lash out and the subsequent need to seek forgiveness for the pain I've inflicted are traits that I and many other Black adults my age have adopted. How do you learn to control your emotions as an adult when you were raised to instinctively deal with anger with violence? And how do you pass on the embarrassment and shame that comes with a whooping to your kids or someone you love?

For the most part, they're punishments that happen in the privacy of your own home. But on the day my mother arrived at Highland Community School (an otherwise-quaint Montessori school that felt like a day care instead of school) and learned that I was "playing Sheneneh," she pulled me out of class and whooped me in the hallway. I returned to class, tears in my eyes, face flushed with embarrassment. I had no idea then that "playing Sheneneh" might make adults think I was acting too feminine or might turn out to be gay. All I knew was that it was no longer okay to act like my favorite TV character.

A week later, that teacher whose name I can't remember asked me to "do Sheneneh" during recess again, as if she hadn't just ratted me out to my mother and watched as I got disciplined in front of my classmates. I declined and spent the rest of my recesses at Highland reading a book alone. I didn't feel like performing anymore. And after a while, I forgot how to. No wonder I was never good enough to be in my high school production of *Footloose*.

Disappear here.

—BRET EASTON ELLIS, *LESS THAN ZERO* (1985)

· · · · ·

HERO TO ZERO

Sometimes your mom drops you off. Other times you catch the bus to school. When you get home, no one's there. You throw on *Batman* or *Power Rangers* and make yourself a snack from the fridge or heat up whatever your mom left you on the stove. You make sure to take the chicken out of the freezer so it can thaw. Most of the time, you forget to actually do this and quickly run the frozen chicken underneath scalding water in the sink before your mom gets home to cook dinner.

My mother couldn't afford a babysitter, so when family friends weren't available, my babysitter was usually a rotating series of Disney movies on VHS. Before you could access every single Disney animated feature on the streaming service Disney+, you had to physically own a Disney film to rewatch it. We didn't have a bookshelf displaying our tastes in literature, but we did have one of those wooden TV consoles that had built-in shelves to display your film collection.

And the most visible titles in that collection were always the Disney films that Mom or my gran or some other relative had bought for my sister and me to watch. If you've seen a VHS tape, you know they usually came in a slim cardboard box that you could slide the VHS out from. But Disney films came in large, pillowy clamshell cases that felt soft and squeezable. Puffy and unnecessarily large boxes that took up a lot of damn space on a shelf but were also immediately recognizable as Disney films, with large, bold lettering on them.

My mom drove the same car for most of my childhood, so I wasn't familiar with the smell of a brand-new car, but I was intimately familiar with the smell of opening a brand-new Disney VHS. Every millennial Disney fan is familiar with that "rip me out the plastic, I been actin' brand new" scent of a new Disney VHS. They smelled like money. Like wealth. And through marketing ploys like the Disney Vault, wherein Disney claimed that their VHS tapes would be returned to after being on sale for a few months to drum up sales and the idea that some titles were scarce, it made every single Disney film you had on your shelf feel like a prized possession. I found myself playing with the VHS boxes just as often as I rewatched *The Little Mermaid* or *Beauty and the Beast*.

The Little Mermaid was released in theaters on November 17, 1989, and it's the first film I have any recollection of seeing in theaters. Most likely, I saw the film at the shuttered-since-2012 Northtown Cinemas. Northtown was on the outskirts of Menomonee Falls, a Milwaukee district for rich white people that I mostly remember for the Kohl's we shopped at for back-to-school clothes. Aside from my predestined queerness, thanks to Ariel being my first cinematic heroine, *The Little Mermaid* was also the beginning of what's been termed the "Disney Renaissance."

If one can point to an era that specifically led to the creation of Disney Adults—grown adults who spend their money on trips to Disney World instead of on drugs and alcohol—it is definitely the Disney Renaissance, which is formally considered to have taken place from November 17, 1989 (the release of *The Little Mermaid*), to June 18, 1999 (the release of *Tarzan*). Unfortunately for the vastly underrated and comedic masterpiece *The Emperor's New Groove*, released in December 2000, it was considered a box office failure and not Renaissance-worthy. However, it did produce a great two-season Disney Channel spin-off series, *The Emperor's New School*. I've watched it while stoned in the past year. It's still funny. Nostalgia isn't always bad!

This decade-long Renaissance produced ten films and garnered Disney a series of accolades. *The Little Mermaid* was the first animated Disney film to get an Academy Award nomination since 1977's *The Rescuers*. "Under the Sea" won composer Alan Menken and lyricist Howard Ashman the Oscar for Best Original Song.

Menken and Ashman, it should be said, are also the team behind *Little Shop of Horrors*, one of my favorite musicals and certainly one of the best musicals in existence not written by Stephen Sondheim. They reunited for *Beauty and the Beast*, which won Disney two Oscars. It's fucked that Ashman died eight months before the release of *Beauty and the Beast* from AIDS complications. But his posthumous Oscar, accepted by his partner, Bill Lauch, was presented by Shirley MacLaine and Liza Minnelli, which just feels like gay history. During their speech, they even shouted out Barbra Streisand as their favorite director and said that they wanted to make a film with her. But unless I missed a part in Streisand's Jonathan Franzen–length memoir *My Name Is Barbra*, that movie never came to fruition. And that feels like a hate crime.

Aladdin (which featured some songs written by Ashman before his death that were ultimately finished by lyricist Tim Rice) won Best Original Score and Best Original Song for "A Whole New World."* Hans Zimmer, who played Coachella the same year as Lady Gaga (this is just an important thing to know, I

---

* Tim Rice is credited for this song, which is a classic, yes, but Ashman's "Friend Like Me," which was also nominated, is the superior song in the film.

think), won his first Oscar writing the score for *The Lion King*. "Can You Feel the Love Tonight" by Elton John and Tim Rice won Best Original Song.

Pocahontas, a truly messy film that rewrites racist colonial history but is also the only whitewashing I will defend with my life, besides the first two albums in Gwen Stefani's solo career, won Menken his final pair of Oscars, which he shares with lyricist Stephen Schwartz.*

The Hunchback of Notre Dame, which is better than you remember, and I know the only things people remember from it are the song "Topsy Turvy" and learning the word "sanctuary," was nominated for Best Original Musical or Comedy Score.

Hercules is a film I adore, but I also need to acknowledge that people are mostly just trying to seem cool when they claim it's the best animated Disney film. It only has three songs anyone actually remembers. One of those songs, "Go the Distance," was nominated for Best Original Song.

Mulan was nominated for Best Original Musical or Comedy Score. Iconic film. Iconic Christina Aguilera song attached to it.

Tarzan closed out the Disney Renaissance with an Oscar win for Phil Collins's "You'll Be in My Heart" for Best Original Song. I actually don't think I've ever seen this film, but I love Phil Collins and men in loincloths.

It wasn't that Walt Disney Animation Studios hadn't produced bangers before. I also grew up heavily obsessed with films like *Peter Pan*, *Alice in Wonderland*, and *One Hundred and One Dalmatians*, but Disney in the nineties gave you *songs*: "Circle of Life," "Poor Unfortunate Souls," "Reflection," "Part of Your World." To

---

* I just felt it necessary to say that Stephen Schwartz's *Wicked* is also one of the best musicals ever written, but, like, somewhere in the top twenty, if I were really bothered to make a list. Points knocked off for "Dear Old Shiz" and "A Sentimental Man," because what was even going on there?

quote a popular Whitney Houston interview sound bite, "You know, songs like that, they are stories that people can identify with. You know what I mean? Anybody! Children were singing [these songs] at graduations, at weddings, at funerals." She was talking about "I Will Always Love You," but she could've just as well been talking about "Friend Like Me"!

In this era, Disney World was heavily promoted not just in commercials, but in synergy with ABC TV shows. The TGIF lineup had episodes of *Family Matters*, *Step by Step*, *Boy Meets World*, and *Full House* take place at Disney World as advertisements for the theme parks. For kids whose parents could afford family vacations, or at least save up enough to afford *one* big family vacation to Disney, these Disney World episodes are what I'm sure have led to the creation of Disney Adults. Disney World was the American dream personified, though the films were all based on fairy tales or myths with much darker endings: In Hans Christian Andersen's original tale, the Little Mermaid kills herself rather than stab the prince to death so she can become a mermaid again, *for instance*. Disney gave you inspirational films straight out of Joseph Campbell's hero's journey, and they were inspirational.

Mom, who used the common Black-mother retort "You got McDonald's money?" when on occasion I would ask if we could have McDonald's for dinner, definitely did not have family-vacation money, so I never grew up with any illusions that I would be visiting Disney World. That was probably for the best. After living in California for a few years, before I moved back to New York City, I decided to finally visit Disney California Adventure Park for the first time and I immediately felt like a kid again, eagerly opening a Disney VHS box and shoving it into the VCR to watch on repeat all afternoon. I left the park having spent over three hundred dollars on merchandise in the gift shop. If I'd ever visited Disney as a teenager, my mother would've gone broke, and I'd absolutely be one of the most annoying Disney Adults you've ever meet.

There are several milestones on the journey to adulthood that you experience in your adolescence. Your mom letting you stay at home by yourself instead of at a neighbor's or relative's house is one of them, but none is bigger than the solo trip, the first time an adult in your life entrusts you to go somewhere on your own. My first such sojourns were out of necessity. If my mom wanted cigarettes, she'd send me to the corner store to pick them up. This eventually evolved into me going on light grocery runs when she didn't feel like doing it, mostly when she wanted someone else to have to use our food stamps instead of her.

I can barely remember my first visit to Northtown Cinemas in 1989, aside from brief flashes of *The Little Mermaid* at age three, but I can vividly recall the first time I attended a movie without adult supervision, and that was on June 11, 1993—when Steven Spielberg's *Jurassic Park* was released. If you're a gay millennial man, then you were obsessed with either Disney or dinosaurs. So while I loved Disney films, I *loved* dinosaurs.

From the moment I first learned in school what dinosaurs were, I became obsessed with them. I had fossil figurines that I assembled in my bedroom. I read books on the various species of dinosaurs. I religiously watched all four seasons of the ABC sitcom *Dinosaurs*, a Jim Henson–produced series about a family of dinosaurs that was essentially a live-action version of *The Simpsons*. The series revolved around the Sinclairs (oddly all different species of dinosaurs, but maybe they were a chosen family), who included working father Earl, stay-at-home mom Fran (voiced by icon Jessica Walter in maybe her oddest role yet, considering she mostly played divas in *Play Misty for Me*, *Arrested Development*, and *Archer*), jock Robbie, nerd Charlene, and Baby, an actual infant dinosaur who was throwing out (probably annoying to any adult watching with me) catchphrases like "I'm the baby, gotta love me!" and "Not the mama!" Baby usually said these lines to Earl before whacking him with a pan.

The final episode of the show, planned as its series finale, showed an ice age fast approaching to kill all the dinosaurs. Ludicrously, people refer to it as the most traumatizing TV finale ever, which, sure. But if you were obsessed with dinosaurs, then you already knew they met their asteroid-induced demise around sixty-six million years prior. In this way, a childhood obsession with dinosaurs was also an obsession with death.

During the weekend of *Jurassic Park*'s release, I was already talking about the film nonstop. The trailer felt cinematic on its own—dinosaurs hatching from eggs, T. rexes and raptors on a rampage. The movie is now considered a classic and one of Spielberg's best. It's not only my favorite Spielberg film but also my favorite film overall. While I have a theory that your favorite Spielberg movie is whichever one you saw when you were between seven and ten years old, *Jurassic Park* still holds up to this day due to the fact that its use of CGI and animatronics makes it appear incredibly realistic.

Not to shit on the CGI of today, but if you watch any current action movie, 90 percent of it looks fake. Nothing about a superhero showdown in a Marvel or DC movie looks remotely real, but when that T. rex escapes from her cage and tries to eat kids Tim and Lex, who are trapped in an unmoving jeep, it's still incredibly visually arresting and scary. It terrified me as a kid as much as it entranced me.

The day my gran drove me to Northtown to see *Jurassic Park* on opening day with one of my best friends, she went to see a different movie. Northtown had eight screens, and movies then stayed in theaters longer than they do now, so it was relatively easy for her to find something else to watch while the kids saw their dinosaur movie. One thing my gran loved was a Whoopi Goldberg comedy. So, most likely, when I saw my dinosaur movie, she was watching the Whoopi Goldberg and Ted Danson comedy *Made in America*, which had been released two weeks prior. In this film, Whoopi's daughter, played by Nia Long, discovers that the sperm donor her mom used to conceive her was not a Black man, like Whoopi'd asked for, but a white one: Ted Danson. Also, Will Smith plays Nia's boyfriend. I'll let you guess whether it's a good movie.

I loved *Jurassic Park* so much after seeing it the first time that I needed to see it again. My gran had run out of movies she was interested in seeing, so she began dropping me off at Northtown by myself every weekend for as long as *Jurassic Park* was in theaters. I needed a dinosaur fix so much that I even rented the incredibly shitty direct-to-video film *Prehysteria!* that was released two weeks after *Jurassic Park*, about a group of baby dinosaurs named after pop musicians. Yes, a movie about miniature dinosaurs named Paula and Madonna and Hammer. It was embarrassing for everyone involved. I'm sure I rented it from Blockbuster at least twenty times.

Jurassic Park had introduced me to newfound independence. I spent time at the movies alone every weekend, watching one of my favorite films, reciting every line, and seeing my favorite dinosaurs rampage through a theme park for two hours. That is, until I was handed the equivalent of a juvenile detention—

I was forced to join the Boys & Girls Club summer camp. It was a day camp, which, in theory, is supposed to enrich kids' lives and personal growth or some bullshit but was mostly just a cheap place for parents to stick their kids during summer so they wouldn't have to be bothered with them in the middle of the day.

Stuck in this camp, I had to quickly relinquish all my new-found independence and endure a new form of bullying. I was a fat kid, yeah, which you learn to deal with throughout the school year by avoiding physical activity in gym glass and holding your books tight to your body when walking through the halls so no one notices the sagging boobs forming on your chest before any of the girls in your class have started wearing a training bra.

But summer camp involved swimming, and it put me on display in a way I had never been before, when I only wanted to sit in a cold movie theater and eat popcorn and drink Mountain Dew.* Not only did I feel trapped by summer camp, but I also felt infantilized. And at the time, I was sporting a hairstyle that may be the only thing in existence worse than a mullet: a rat tail. It wasn't an Eddie Murphy–in–*Coming to America*–level Zamunda tail, but more of a little puff-tuft-in-the-back kind.

In the mid-eighties to the early nineties, it became popular for boys to have mostly close-cropped hair with one bit left to grow long at the back of their head. I don't recall any other Black students at school having this hairstyle or why the adults in my family found it "cute," but the minute I was at summer camp, it became another thing for other kids to mock me for, and I hated it.

---

* Everyone who grew up in Milwaukee in the nineties loved Mountain Dew; this is an irrefutable fact.

Until I was eighteen, the only barbershop Gran would take me to was Sid's Shear Magic Hair Styles on West Hopkins, run by family friend Sidney. I remember the place vividly. It had a big bright white sign outside with red lettering that hadn't been changed since the seventies. It looked reminiscent of a store-front from old episodes of *Sesame Street* or *The Electric Company*.

Before straight Black men used podcasts to share their dubious opinions on pop culture, politics, sports, sex, and gender roles, they did so in barbershops. There's been enough written by straight Black men about how these spaces were safe havens and by queer Black men about how they felt uncomfortable expressing their queerness in such a heteronormative space.

For me, who hated leaving the house and would much rather be watching TV or reading a book, being at the barbershop was its own special kind of torture that involved my gran catching up with Sid and whoever else happened to be at the shop that day while I flipped through issues of *Jet* or *Ebony* on days I'd forgotten a book, and tried to keep myself occupied until Sid was ready to cut my hair. Somehow, even with an appointment, I always had to wait at least an hour before Sid cut my hair. Most of the time, Gran would leave me while she was running errands, which meant that when I was done, I'd have to sit there and wait for her to return while feigning small talk with adults and pretending I was at all interested in which swimsuit model was the *Jet* Beauty of the Week.

But try as I might to vanquish that rat tail each time, Gran would always come back just before Sid could cut it, reminding me how cute she found it and how devastated she'd be if I got rid of it. So, I smiled and grinned and bore the hairstyle I had grown to loathe over the summer of 1993.

Until some point later in those months, when the Boys &

Girls camp came up with the idea of a field trip that just involved going to the movies. The teenagers were going to see *Jurassic Park*, and the younger kids were being forced to watch some wack *FernGully* rip-off called *Once Upon a Forest*. *Once Upon a Forest*'s plot revolves around three animal children who try to cure one of their friends, who's been poisoned by pollution fumes. I'm sure it was cute for the other children at summer camp, but I had just turned seven, and I was officially too old to watch a bunch of talking animals, or "Furlings," save their friend from chemical cancer.

Unfortunately, *Jurassic Park* was rated PG-13, and the camp counselors refused to let me see it, even though I could recite the dialogue by heart because I'd watched it "twenty goddamn times," to quote Drew Barrymore in *Scream* insisting on how many times she'd seen *Friday the 13th*. I was forced to sit with the rest of the babies (who were probably seven like me, as that was the youngest you could be to join, but had any of those bitches read a Michael Crichton novel like I had?) and watch *Once Upon a Forest*.

I was livid. I felt like all the progress I'd made toward adulthood was gone. I was the opposite of Herc in *Hercules*, I'd gone from hero to *zero*. And so, to regain control of my life in the only way I knew how, the next time I was in Sid's chair (and my gran had gone to run errands), I told him to chop that fucking rat tail off my head before she got back.

BRITNEY SPEARS: I really do like Pepsi. I really do.
TUCKER CARLSON: Really? What's your favorite kind?
BRITNEY SPEARS: My favorite kind of Pepsi? Pepsi's Pepsi.

—CNN (2003)

· · · · ·

OPRAH RUINED MY LIFE

One day, Oprah will pay for her crimes. I'm not talking about making snake oil salesmen like Drs. Oz and Phil famous or the 2018 film adaptation of *A Wrinkle in Time*; I'm talking about her documentation of her weight-loss from the nineties until now. If you were born in the nineties, then Oprah has pretty much been the same size for most of your adolescence and adulthood. But for elder millennials, born in 1986 or earlier, and anyone older, Oprah's journey with her weight has a very specific choke hold on you.

Oprah's weight-loss odyssey began with the November 15, 1988, episode (titled "Diet Dreams Come True") of her daytime talk show *The Oprah Winfrey Show*, when she announced that she'd dropped a significant amount of weight in four months. With a feathered bob and dressed in a size 10 pair of Calvin Klein jeans, black boots with a sexy but sensible heel, a glittery belt, and a body-hugging black sweater, Oprah looked like your auntie who let you go to the corner store to buy her Newports rather than the oversize-blazer-and-pantsuit-wearing middle-school science teacher she'd formerly resembled. And to further drive home the fact that she'd lost a lot of weight, she rolled out the exact amount in animal fat on a little red wagon.

She wasn't just hosting *The Oprah Winfrey Show*; she was *doing* shows, honey. Oprah was showing out, and as a result, "Diet Dreams Come True" became the highest-rated episode of the program's twenty-five-year history (and it remains so).

Oprah has since expressed regret over this moment. In 2024, she hosted ABC's *An Oprah Special: Shame, Blame and the Weight Loss Revolution* to discuss her use of Ozempic, the antidiabetic medication also used for weight loss, and how she finally conquered her struggles with weight. In the special, she blames the media for bullying her into trying fad diets, starving herself, etc., over the years, and how much shame she has for carting out that wagon of animal fat. In fact, she started to gain the weight back the day after shooting "Diet Dreams Come True."

I'm not here to hold Oprah to some moral standard that I don't even hold myself to—I used a version of Ozempic prescribed to me in 2023. It worked well for a few months, until the Writers Guild of America strike happened and I ran out of money for it (and a gym membership), even with the discount from my insurance, so that was the end of that! The only issue I have with Oprah discussing her weight shame and then doing a special about how Ozempic finally helped her is how it's really only about helping *her*. Which would be fine if the whole point of her talk show was about helping people. Every time she discussed weight over the years, it was all to justify to the public why she was on the latest fad diet. With Oprah, when there's something to sell, objectivity always seems to go out the window.

The Oprah Winfrey Show debuted on September 8, 1986, and Oprah's brand of an emotional, relatable talk show ran alongside the highly rated news and tabloid talk shows of that era. Now daytime TV mostly consists of Kelly Clarkson singing

covers of popular songs, Drew Barrymore talking about whatever's trending on the internet three weeks after you've already
discovered it, and inexplicably, *Maury*, which has been running
since 1991 and is essentially the classier version of *Jerry Springer*.
On *Maury*, poor and working-class people cry and taunt one
another over romantic affairs and paternity scandals. On *Jerry
Springer*, those same people have fistfights. *Maury*, which will
forever be remembered in pop culture for Povich's delivery of
"You are *not* the father!" (or less often "You *are* the father!")
after a paternity test, is an incredibly boring show otherwise.
Jerry Springer, on the other hand, is art.

Oprah's program, however, became incredibly influential
because she sold relatability and not a sideshow. In 2002, *Christianity Today* described how she'd essentially become a spiritual
leader to her viewers. Her friends became their new mentors.
Dr. Phil became their therapist. Suze Orman became their fi-
nancial planner. Dr. Oz became their doctor. Iyanla Vanzant
became their life coach. Whatever books Oprah read, the people read. This backfired after author James Frey was revealed to
have fabricated or exaggerated parts of his memoir *A Million
Little Pieces*, which was an Oprah's Book Club pick. To save
face, she invited him on the show for a public tongue-lashing. I
don't even remember if Oprah uttered the words "I feel like I
have been duped" to Frey, but I always remember her saying
them, so they're real enough for me. Oprah taught me to go
with what I feel, even if it's not necessarily the truth. Oprah
could convince us to do anything—and this authority commu-
nicated a warm relatability. Inexplicably, she became everyone
in America's weight-loss guru because Americans are experts at
taking personal anecdotes as facts.

What Oprah hasn't truly apologized for is that when she

rolled sixty-seven pounds of animal fat into millions of homes[*] through their TVs, she sparked an entire generation of unhealthy dieters. It was about fighting the media's depiction of her, yeah, but there's a reason Oprah's Book Club selections sell out immediately. She has the Midas touch. But, sis, you know you were in physical pain with each and every fad diet you went on, yet you still went on TV and suggested other people try them. Maybe Oprah's misery wanted some company: "If I have to starve myself to look good, then, shit, so does everyone else."

I was a fat kid. And being a fat kid in the nineties involved constant in-your-face reminders of it. Celebrities like Britney Spears and Jessica Simpson were called fat even when they were rail-thin. Every TV sitcom had a fat-friend character whose only dialogue involved responding to punch lines about their weight—Countess Vaughn's Kim Parker on the UPN sitcom *Moesha* got at least one fat joke an episode devoted to her until she was freed with a spin-off series, *The Parkers*, which starred her and Mo'Nique. As the stars of their own sitcom, both women received the gift of *multiple* fat jokes an episode.

Middle school was a minefield of not just the jokes, but also the everyday interactions that reminded people of your existence. I think that for most fat kids during this period, before "body positivity" or the democratization of normal-looking people hopping on TikTok and going viral, there was a constant need to hide. Of course, there are still the constant thinspo and workout videos

---

[*] The year 1988 is too early for me to have a memory of this, but the number of times I saw it replayed through archival footage on pop-culture TV shows of the *I Love the '80s* variety made it clear that this was Oprah's villain arc.

that creep into everyone's algorithms and bring back the worst aspects of nineties diet culture. As an adult, I'm consciously aware of the tricks.

The shame I once felt as a kid, ordering the weight-loss pills Hydroxycut after seeing late-night TV ads, would no longer be a secret today. We watch both influencers and friends publicly and rapidly shed weight due to injecting themselves with Ozempic or similar drugs used for weight-loss. Oprah herself recently embraced weight-loss medication on the cover of *People*, insisting that she was taking back the narrative of her weight loss. Anti-fatness is now much more polite. Everyone you know posts a selfie at the gym every day, and if you don't, you wonder if people think you're committed to never looking hot. Ozempic allegedly makes you shit like crazy. Which should be no surprise; Hydroxycut had me racing to the third-floor bathroom during a theology class because I had to shit my brains out every day while I took it.

In middle school, I became the antonym of Ralph Ellison's ideology in *Invisible Man*, wherein I *didn't* want people to see me. I hated gym class because people could see me fail at running, being out of breath, and tugging at my T-shirt so it didn't conform to the fat on my body. I hid behind my Coke-bottle glasses and the latest Goosebumps book so kids would see me as a nerd, not Augustus Gloop from *Willy Wonka & the Chocolate Factory*.

It was the nineties, so I could hide in baggy off-brand JCPenney clothes. Not just because my family was on a budget, but because the one time I tried to fit in with the other kids at school and wear a FUBU shirt I saved up my allowance for, the first thing I heard in homeroom was "Look at Ira in his FUBU!" The anxiety that came from being on display overrode the knowledge that pointing out a piece of clothing someone's wearing is how Black people compliment one another. But language is fun, because the same phrase can also work as an insult, depending on the tone. "Shut up, FUBU" works just as easily, knocking someone down by acknowledging a piece of clothing they're wearing in a negative tone.

In fact, what got me to stop wearing the FUBU shirt was a substitute gym teacher who refused to call me by any name other than FUBU, but pronounced "FU-BEW."* Substitute teachers are often the cruelest people in middle school! Besides her, there was also one blond late-twenties English substitute (who gave white-ally energy) who read a horror novel I'd written in fourth grade that was set in an amusement park. She never returned to school after I gave it to her. If she hated it that much, she could've at least given me the pages back! (I have no recollection of why that was my only copy of the novel.)

By the time I got to high school, my insecurities increased. At least up until middle school, I was with predominantly Black kids. I was fat, but so were others, or at least other people in their families were too. I was uncomfortable about how I looked, but not as much as I was when my mom and Gran made me go to Marquette University High School. Never mind that this all-boys school terrified me as a closeted fourteen-year-old because whenever I told people I was going there instead of Rufus King, where most of my friends and classmates were going, they lowered their voices and said, in hushed tones, "Ain't that the *gay* school?" like I'd just admitted I watched *Friends* instead of *Martin* on Thursday nights. For the record, my uncle Bill's partner, Kevin, introduced me to both shows during Thanksgiving one year. Kevin was Black,

---

* Now that 2000s trends are in again, I wear vintage FUBU clothing I find online. I'm reclaiming that shit.

but he and my uncle were both Chicago-living bougie Black gay men in the nineties, and I suppose that meant you watched NBC and not Fox on Thursday nights.

The majority of the students at Marquette were naturally skinny or had athletic bodies, since Marquette was known for its athletics as much as its educational program, so I was all of a sudden thrust into a school with a bunch of white teenage boys as I was not only trying to figure out my gay shit but also growing resentful of how a social calendar of TV and books and sneaking snacks and sodas in the middle of the night without waking anyone had turned my body into what it was. Fear of physical exertion and showering with a group of boys who I was attracted to and had bodies I envied kept me dodging the football coach at Marquette, who routinely attempted to get me to try out for the team. The athletes worked out in our Equinox-level gym every morning, which I also avoided because I had no idea what "working out" meant.

Marquette had a dress code of collared shirts during the week and shirts and ties on special occasions, because this was a respectable *white* school, which meant that baggy clothes were *out*. My FUBU shirt was *definitely* out, although by this time, Justin Timberlake was wearing FUBU, and the hockey team at Marquette listened to more hip-hop music than I did. Most of my classmates wore polos as their collared-shirt option. Polos are my least favorite type of shirt. Even at my skinniest, I have never possessed the figure, or the arms, frankly, for a polo. One thing they do is highlight your chest, and I didn't have pecs in high school so much as a chest that most women would pay Dr. Miami thousands for. A chest I tried to hide with a belt tied around it every school day for three years until one day in the car, my mother hugged me and asked what I was wearing a belt under my shirt for. She stopped short of further inquiry after I gave her a look, because if my family is good at one thing, it's not asking questions that probably *should* be asked.

Oprah lost her sixty-seven pounds by running up that treadmill like Kate Bush. She also did it by essentially starving herself with a diet of Optifast, a protein power mixed with water. A diet like that sounds insane now, but growing up in the nineties meant you were always inundated with diets like this on infomercials or in magazine ads. While nowadays there are at least enough people claiming to be trainers and dieticians on Instagram to make you aware that exercise and healthy eating habits are the way to lose weight, I grew up with none of that. My family has always been concerned with their weight, whether it be Gran, my mom, or my sister at various points in their lives, but in the nineties, it was mostly "let's eat better" and maybe "let's use the treadmill that's in the basement."

Now, when I can afford to, I pay a personal trainer to motivate me to work out, but as a high schooler who'd rather be doing anything other than working out, I was not compelled to go downstairs and walk on the treadmill every day. The extent of my workout routine consisted of my two-mile Saturday walks to and from Collector's Edge Comics on 78th and Burleigh that would often be supplemented by a seven-and-a-half-inch Italian special from Cousins. This Milwaukee-based sub store is *far* superior to Jimmy John's and Subway. Not that I'm not also a Subway enthusiast (which is maybe the most basic thing about me, aside from my love of California Pizza Kitchen), having gone to high school and college at the height of Jared Fogle's Subway campaign.

To understand how much the nineties wrecked our brains

when it came to diets, once we reached the 2000s, it was commonplace to acknowledge how ridiculous fad diets were but also to conjure up some reason why they _might_ work, because that is how you sold health magazines. Fogle lost 245 pounds by exercising and eating a diet of Subway sandwiches in the late nineties. In 1999, a former friend of Jared's wrote an article on his Subway diet for the _Indiana Daily Student_, and _Men's Health_ included him in an article titled "Stupid Diets That Work." Soon enough, Subway picked up on the story and started featuring him in ads with a disclaimer about how Fogle accomplished his weight loss with the Subway diet but also with "a lot of walking."

If you ask anyone who watched these commercials as they aired, I guarantee very few, if any, will remember what the Subway diet consisted of. The commercials didn't point out that Jared only ate a small turkey sub, one large veggie sub, baked potato chips, and diet soda, equaling about two thousand calories a day. Fogle's initial Subway commercials involved him leaving his house in the middle of the day, inexplicably dressed for the office, and stopping at his local Subway before staring at a window advertisement that touts Subway as having "seven subs with six grams of fat or less." The subs in the window advertisement are all six-inch subs, but Jared purchases a footlong and eats on a park bench. At no point does the commercial indicate which of the subs have six grams of fat or less or which one Jared even buys, because that's not the point of a commercial anyway.

As Don Draper said, "People want to be told what to do so badly that they'll listen to anyone." Diet crazes aren't inherently about dieting so much as shortcuts to looking and feeling better. They exist because people want the end result without having to put in the work. So when you show a before picture of Jared and then show him having lost 245 pounds by eating at Subway, you're telling customers to walk to Subway and eat a sub every day, and they can lose weight too.

Most people following the Subway diet were not eating any damn veggie subs. I certainly wasn't. I loved anything without veggies, like the Italian BMT (which Subway's Hong Kong website claims meant "biggest, meatiest, and tastiest," but it was allegedly named after the Brooklyn–Manhattan Transit system in New York) or the Spicy Italian, the "As-Salaam Alaykum, no oink for me" version of the BMT. (It's the same sandwich minus the Black Forest ham.) This is partly because the lettuce at Subway is quite possibly the worst thing I have ever tasted, so I stopped adding it to my subs. I can't *recall* if spinach has always been readily available at Subway, but I know I didn't start adding it to my subs, along with tomatoes and peppers, until college. I'm going to pretend that, like me, Subway didn't discover spinach until the mid-2000s.

The fact that the Subway diet was misleading shouldn't be shocking; this was from the era that made people believe that Special K cereal, which boasted having "real fruit" mixed in with whole-grain cereal, was going to change the trajectory of their lives. It was advertised as a diet food, one that could transform an unhappy, sexless housewife into a cheerful, skinny white woman simply by eating cereal. In 1980, Kellogg's released a commercial introducing the "Special K pinch," wherein a housewife knew that if she pinched more than an inch of fat on her waist, she needed to watch her weight. Her not-at-all-skinny husband chuckles, "I bet I know what you're having for breakfast!"

By the nineties, models were eating Special K while wearing bikinis. SlimFast used the same promotional methods and made you think it was a perfectly reasonable substitute for breakfast, lunch, and dinner. My gran's kitchen was *stocked* with SlimFast. I think the Subway marketing team should've been hired by the government to promote vaccines during the pandemic, because to this day, people still remember the Subway diet and not the fact that Jared Fogle is currently serving a fifteen-year prison sentence for possession of child pornography.

When you were a kid and your parents were on a diet, that meant *you* were on a diet too, and because of her Pepsi addiction, my gran didn't allow soda in the house. For most of my developing years, she was ostensibly my mother. I lived with her, and she raised me from adolescence. Another thing you should know is that she was addicted to Pepsi. Yes, Pepsi is addictive. Gran's addiction wasn't unexpected, given that she doesn't drink alcohol. I get my dopamine doses from drugs and alcohol while she gets hers from that chilled red-white-and-blue can that often replaced water during the day and at meals.

Pepsi's advertising team is as much the GOAT as Subway's. Pepsi has always tasted worse than Coke, but somehow, I don't associate Coca-Cola with cool; I associate them with polar bears at the North Pole thanks to their annual Christmas ads. Every celebrity from the nineties and aughts has been part of a Pepsi campaign since Michael Jackson's 1985 commercial aired a year before I was born. The Pepsi logo was on display much brighter than Coca-Cola's at the corner store near my house. My teen dream Britney Spears kept "The Joy of Pepsi" in my head long after the 2001 Super Bowl commercial. In 2013, I woke up at five a.m. just to watch Beyoncé's surprise announcement that ended up being a Pepsi commercial (which was not as evil as the time she had me watching *Good Morning America* to announce she was going vegan for like a month).

Gran grew up during Jim Crow in Tiptonville, Tennessee, a town of fewer than two thousand. Until then, the only images of Black people in advertising consisted of racist slave carica-tures like Aunt Jemima and Uncle Ben. In the 1940s, new Pepsi president Walter Mack realized there was an opportunity to market to Black people differently. The cynic in me knows that capitalism will always find a way to exploit Black people, but I want to think that the reportedly progressive Mack also be-lieved that Pepsi had an opportunity to course-correct the of-fensive caricatures used by Pepsi's marketing team. He hired Black sales executive Edward Boyd, and Boyd helped usher in an era of an all-Black Pepsi marketing team who weathered the KKK and the racism of their own co-workers in the South as they defied segregation and Jim Crow laws to market directly to Black people. The ads themselves became more reminiscent of the family-centered TV sitcoms that would soon dominate the airwaves in the fifties.

Is it any wonder, then, that aggressively marketing an aspi-rational image of Blackness led to an uptick in sales and to my adolescent gran looking at a Pepsi can in a much more favor-able light than that other soda that 3D renderings of polar bears drank in commercials? Years later, marketing executives would use images of cool Blackness to market Newport cigarettes to my mother's generation. There's certainly no altruism in getting a generation of Black women and men addicted to nicotine.

Newport ads in *Jet* and *Ebony* magazines and the packs my mom smoked in the car while listening to nineties hip-hop were my childhood blueprint of what "cool and Black" meant. The ubiquitous green-and-white lettering associated with Newport print ads included images of Black people playing basketball, at cookouts, and even skiing. They wanted the bougie niggas smoking menthols too!

To this day, the colors remain iconic. And because Newports were popular among Black people, they became popular among white people who wanted to seem cool too. Hell, even Rob Lowe's Billy Hicks smoked menthol cigarettes in *St. Elmo's Fire*. Billy also played the saxophone, lived in a rough part of town, and had a kid out of wedlock. The Brat Pack played a lot of nigga-coded white characters, when you think about it. Duckie in *Pretty in Pink* dressed exactly like Little Richard and sang Otis Redding. The recent documentary *Brats* (which I was interviewed for) dove into how upset Andrew McCarthy was that he carried the "Brat Pack" label with him throughout his career, but I think more than a few Black actors would've loved to have had that label and recognition along with the chance to get paid to smoke some of their aunties' favorite cigarettes on film.

Aside from the marketing to Black people, Newports are also popular because they're menthols. All kids do now is smoke flavored vapes, which is a direct descendant of kids puffing on menthol cigarettes in the nineties. In 2022, the American Health Association published a report on the cigarette industry's decades-long push to sell menthols to women, kids, and Black people. The tactics included Black celebrity endorsements, handing out samples and discount coupons in predominantly Black neighborhoods, and flooding urban areas with menthol ads on billboards, buses, and subways.

Kids like shit with flavor. It's why we prefer Frosted Flakes for breakfast. The popularity of menthols and flavored vapes among teenagers is why the government has started cracking down on the sale of them. You can't even get Newports with menthol in Los Angeles anymore. Another reason I had to leave! New York still lets me buy the menthol cigarettes I want despite their addictive nature to teens. Like the Michael Jordan internet meme, New York said, "Fuck them kids."

When I picked up smoking again, in my vagabond-expat-writing-a-book-in-Europe phase (Amsterdam, specifically, which lasted about six months, and I wrote maybe three of this book's essays there), I returned to the United States and started smoking Newports, partially because of those memories of my mom smoking them, but also because the advertising is forever ingrained in my mind. When other people ask me for a cigarette, it's done with a pleasant look of surprise that I'm smoking one and an eagerness to mask the cancer they're inhaling with a coat of nostalgia. Not to generalize all Black people as loving Newports, though! At a party once, I offered a friend a cigarette, and she looked me dead in the face and said, "Ira, I'm not smoking no damn Newports."

Not that I'm promoting smoking. My love of Newports doesn't mean you need to go and pick up a packet of Newports. You see, my addiction has nothing to do with you! But my gran's Pepsi addiction had everything to do with me. So, she told me that I could still drink it, but I had to keep it hidden away from her in the house. In retrospect, this probably saddled me with my fraught relationship with food and dieting (the idea of merely keeping something—anything—"hidden" would be enough to change your habits). For her part, Oprah has recently come out as using a form of the antidiabetic drug Ozempic to maintain her weight. The recent honesty in her journey is commendable, even if she still views it only as the result of having been attacked in the media for her weight and not part of a media narrative of herself and America that she also contributed to.

Gran and I were both hiding things then—coming out to Gran was more frightening to me than coming out to the mother I had a strained relationship with and the father I hadn't even seen since I was ten. But it was always something I'd planned to do. Those plans usually involved telling her well after high school. Maybe when I introduced her to a boyfriend, my sexual orientation would seem normal. I did have my uncle Bill and his partner, Kevin. But my uncle died in the nineties, as did most of the would-be gay elders of his generation, and a living example who should've made it easier for me to grow up into a man comfortable loving other men publicly was taken from me. Moments of grief can form our identities, even if it's not our own grief. Much like most painful events in my family, the details of my uncle's death weren't discussed with me, out of my family's grief over the loss, so I've had no connection to Bill's life other than a few offhand "You remind me of him" comments from family members that were clearly subconscious ways of their minds figuring out that I might be gay too.

Luckily, since I'm a millennial born in the late eighties, my queer education would come from the internet. During my high school days, internet porn wasn't as available as it is now. Before Twitter, OnlyFans, or even Instagram Stories shared with close friends, there were websites like Sean Cody. But my family shared one computer, and I'd already been outed as reading X-rated *Buffy* fanfic where the Slayer fucked her Watcher, Giles—so my solution to not getting caught watching porn was to buy a DVD and have it shipped it to my house. It might be hard to remember your teenage decision-making skills now, but our logic—no matter how Mad Hatter—made all the sense in the world to us. The DVD in question was a parody of the Naomi Watts horror film *The Ring,* from back when she still made good choices about films to star in (what the fuck is a Penguin Bloom?!). It was called *The Hole,* and if you've seen *Million Dollar Listing* (which I personally haven't, because I don't want to watch men sell real estate), you'll probably recognize former porn star and current Bethenny Frankel reality TV sidekick Fredrik Eklund (who was known as Tag Eriksson then).

I managed to sneak the DVD past Gran and into my room without her asking any questions. I'm sure I told her the DVD was *Buffy*-related. I hid it in my room while I was at school, but absentmindedly. I hid it where I was also hiding . . . the Pepsi that Gran swore she didn't want to drink anymore. One day I came home from school, and Gran was sitting in our living room. She said, "We need to talk." I had no idea what she meant until I dropped my backpack off in my room and found *The Hole* lying in plain sight on my bed. Could I have been that much of an idiot to have just left it out like that? Then I realized that, no, I couldn't have been. "You were snooping in my room?" I asked, taking the offense. "I wasn't trying to spy on you," she insisted. "I was looking for a Pepsi, and I know you keep them in your room." Never trust anyone who says they're on a diet.

Gran asked if there was anything I wanted to tell her. And here's where I could've come out and ended my high school turmoil of pretending not to be attracted to boys while attending an all-boys school, like some Sisyphean torment. Besides, it was clear she already knew. She had a gay brother, so it didn't take more than having read a couple Nancy Drew books in her youth to figure it out.

But instead, I said, "I was going to plant it in the locker of someone I hate." And you know what? She believed me. By that point in high school, I'd already tried to rig a school election . . . twice . . . and pretended I'd been mugged to get out of taking a theology exam. I was practically Bart Simpson. So, Ira being up to another scam wasn't altogether shocking. "How did you even buy this DVD?" she asked. This is when I had to admit I'd used an old credit card of hers I'd found buried in a drawer. That's what pissed her off, so she snatched up the DVD and said she was returning it.

The next day, I arrived home from school with the same DVD resting on my bed. "I couldn't return it," she said, appearing in my doorway. "So, you can keep it. You know . . . if you want it." This was, of course, her way of asking if all her instincts telling her that I was gay like her brother, my uncle Bill, and his partner, Kevin, were right, because at this point, I was certainly watching *Friends* and *Seinfeld* on Thursday nights. And after all, I did go to "the gay school," even if she was the one who sent me there in the first place. I shrugged and didn't have a response. Which, I suppose, in my own way, is how I came out to the most important person in my life. But also, as I said before: If my family is good at one thing, it's not asking questions.

We are human, or whatever.

— DARIA MORGENDORFFER, *DARIA* (1999)

· · · · ·

I'M NOT DARIA

I always thought I was Daria.

Daria was an animated series that aired on MTV in the late nineties starring sarcastic, nihilistic teenager Daria Morgendorffer. I watched it amid Britney Spears and Destiny's Child music videos and episodes of *The Real World* and *Road Rules*. Created by Glenn Eichler and Susie Lewis, it was a spin-off of Mike Judge's *Beavis and Butt-Head*, an early-nineties animated series that exists as one of those pop-culture markers that delineates Gen X from millennials.

When Gen X thinks about their favorite nineties MTV cartoon, it's usually *Beavis and Butt-Head*. Rife with sex and fart jokes amid frequent pop-culture references, it was perfect for adolescent boys and stoned college students. Thankfully, as a late-eighties millennial, I missed the boat on having to care about *Beavis and Butt-Head*, a show I've never found particularly funny. Despite my affinity for wearing flannel and Doc Martens, that era of culture, dominated by *Wayne's World* and Bill & Ted, offers nothing for my interests. Those were comedies predicated on identifying with straight, white protagonists who were idiots.[*] But *Daria*, on the other hand, mocked those kinds of protagonists.

---

[*] Though for some reason, I fucking love the movie *Mallrats*, which is of the same genre.

Daria was for the teenagers who thought they were the smartest person in any room. Teenagers who were less inclined to rebel against authority were more likely to possess antipathy toward authority figures because they're idiots. Daria's parents, Helen and Jake, are former hippies who gave up their Hanoi Jane* aspirations and joined corporate America. Helen is mostly self-involved, and Jake shouts a lot, and while they're not exactly stupid (well, Jake is), they often fail miserably at being parents.†

The dumbest adults on *Daria* are often the teachers at her school. There's Principal Angela Li, who's more corrupt than stupid, but she is a deeply unserious woman. She is less interested in helping her students than making a quick buck off them, as seen in the episode where Li decides to fix Lawndale High's lack of football equipment (never mind the school's failing in providing basic educational equipment to students and teachers) by signing an advertisement deal with Ultra Cola. The school is bombarded with extra vending machines and ads for Ultra Cola, but when the students refuse to drink the soda, she stalks around the school with an axe, tearing open the vending machines to make students drink the product.

Then there's Mr. O'Neill, an overly emotional English teacher. He's one of the few teachers who seems to care about Daria's well-being, even if his abundance of sentiment is saccharine and naive. Daria seems to have a soft spot for him in most episodes, or at least she realizes that her withering barbs are probably a bit too much for Mr. O'Neill and his anxious fragility. After all, English

---

* A nickname given to actress Jane Fonda during her anti-war protests in Vietnam.

† There's one episode where Daria's mother defends her daughter's right to make a school art project with a bulimia joke in it, but that was an exception to the rule that Helen was an awful mother.

teachers are usually the favorite teacher of every queer or outcast kid in high school. Learning about depression and anxiety and other human emotions through *The Catcher in the Rye* is often your first bit of armor in the real world.

A committed English teacher could help you develop a very important real-world skill: one-liners as a defense mechanism. At those, nobody was better than Daria. You could imagine spouting one of her best quips ("I don't have low self-esteem; I have low esteem for everyone else," "My biggest fear right now is that I'll wake up and this conversation won't be a dream") to whatever equivalent of the Fashion Club existed at your school. The Fashion Club was a clique at Daria's high school, Lawndale, concerned with "looking good" that would've scared the Plastics. Regina George might be a bitch, but Fashion Club head honcho Sandi Griffin is a cunt, and, well, to paraphrase Tiffany "New York" Pollard,* cunt next to bitch, cunt is gonna devour bitch.

I went to an all-boys' school pre-*Glee*, during the first George W. Bush administration, so I had no *direct* equivalent of the Fashion Club, though maybe I'd have come out earlier if I were inspired by a clique of bitchy homosexuals driving their parents' Porsches and wearing Hollister jeans and puka-shell necklaces. That was the height of Milwaukee fashion in the early 2000s, I fear.

The closest thing to superficial, brain-dead nemeses at my school were Conclave, the student body government at Marquette High. It was a collection of rich kids with type-A personalities like Reese Witherspoon in *Election*. Every year, the seniors put on a show called *Follies*, where they parodied the

---

* Describing a romantic rival on *Flavor of Love*, New York once said, "She's a cute girl. But cute next to gorgeous, gorgeous is gonna devour cute."

school and its teachers. Our class, who in retrospect put on a horribly offensive production, depicted Conclave as Nazis with the letter *C* replacing the swastika on their armbands. And we had them sing a parody of "Springtime for Hitler" from the musical *The Producers*. That's just a notch below the brownface the theater department put on white students so they could portray Puerto Ricans in *West Side Story* and Incas in *The Royal Hunt of the Sun*.

The gift of a good high school English teacher is that their wholehearted earnestness is often enough to make you repent your teenage nihilism. Despite his penchant for being annoying, Mr. O'Neill often attempted to inspire Daria to channel her unique art rather than comment on life from the sidelines. The irony in that, of course, is that most disaffected teens who spend their lives being an inactive participant in high school life eventually *do* channel their work into art. This is how freelance culture critics are made. This is a self-drag.

There are three pivotal English teachers from high school who made me who I am today. The first was Ms. Halston, who taught freshman English and Shakespeare plays. She was my first introduction to *theater*, pronounced with the kind of annoying inflection you develop in a BFA program. *Julius Caesar* was my first introduction to Shakespeare—thank God, otherwise the "we should totally just stab Caesar!" scene from *Mean Girls* wouldn't hit as hard.

Not to jump into an astrology diversion, but did you know that Julius Caesar was a Cancer? Easily the most annoying astrological sign for a man to have, so it makes sense that Caesar's friends would eventually get sick of him and stab him to death.

Another thing about Caesar is he's one of history's best stunt queens, and I firmly believe that reading this Shakespeare play before any other will spark an unending love of camp and spectacle. You're actually predestined to become a theater fag if your introduction to it is *Julius Caesar*. Conversely, suppose your introduction to theater is *Romeo and Juliet*. In that case, chances are you hung posters of Marilyn Monroe and Audrey Hepburn on your dorm walls and lived, laughed, and loved yourself into becoming a bad writer.

Unfortunately, Ms. Halston was kind of mean, and though I do admire an austere teacher (very Trunchbull in *Matilda*), I have never been a fan of austere authority figures. I didn't gag for the Trunchbull in *Matilda*, and I certainly didn't need her teaching English! She never once cast me in one of the winter plays that she directed, and then for *Follies*, when I auditioned to portray the one Black teacher in our school, she cast a white student who talked in a jive accent.

One time I returned to school after going broke in Los Angeles and being forced to spend several months back at home in Milwaukee, working at Macy's in the women's shoe department. I tried to recapture my high school glory, like an aging quarterback with an injury who still shows up at homecoming games, and offered to help out with the winter play. I visited school and cornered Ms. Halston and offered her my services. And then she never responded to any of my emails. Turns out, I had no high school glory. And maybe I was more annoying in high school than I thought, like Liz Lemon on *30 Rock* realizes she was during her high school reunion. Realizing you were the villain in your high school teacher's story is maybe the hardest pill you'll ever have to swallow.

The second pivotal teacher was Mr. Elliott, who was working an uphill battle because, as incoming freshmen, our entire class was assigned Lance Armstrong's *It's Not About the Bike*. I hate Lance Armstrong. Not because of the doping and drug trafficking, which, if we're being honest, would make Lance very likable if he were the star of a prestige TV drama, but because he did Sheryl Crow dirty (being awful to the woman who made the song "Soak Up the Sun" should be punishable by death, actually) and because I really, truly hate his fucking memoir. I still have PTSD from every boy on an athletic team at MUHS wearing those ugly yellow Livestrong bracelets. Seeing Jacob Elordi wear one in the mid-2000s period piece *Saltburn* gave me war flashbacks.

Despite being forced to talk about Armstrong at length for the first few weeks of class, we eventually moved on to reading other things. I can't even remember what else we read in his class, but I do have very fond memories of Mr. Elliott attempting to relate to me by referencing pop culture in his tests and quizzes. Usually, they were about *Friends* (I forgive him; he was white and in his late twenties) or *Seinfeld*. And the sweetest, most Mr. O'Neill thing I know about him is that he was the moderator for the secret gay–straight alliance in school. I only heard about it through whispers since I wasn't out then, but one of my best friends at the time, Luke, became a member after he came out on a school retreat called Kairos.

Kairos is a Christian retreat where students went their junior year to deepen their faith and relationship with God. It takes place over a weekend, and you share your own personal story and discover personal stories from all the other attendees. Our class went in separate groups throughout the year, and the stories were supposed to stay secret, but coming out at Kairos isn't exactly a thing that stays secret in high school, so I knew about Luke's "yep, I'm gay!" moment before he could even come out to me himself.

You'd think my best friend coming out would've given me the courage to do the same when I went on the retreat myself. The personal story I probably should've shared is that I too was gay, but I wasn't about to do all of *that*. Luke wasn't exactly given a Pride parade for coming out! And that supposed safe haven of Kairos was also where another classmate's confession was that he secretly hated Black people. Not particularly shocking coming from a white football player from Wisconsin but also not particularly inviting for me to introduce myself to the school as not just the Black one, but the *gay* Black one.

The third pivotal teacher was my sophomore English teacher, Mr. Collins. Maybe the *most* pivotal in becoming who I am today. This is because I was in love with Mr. Collins. He was a Jesuit—the "cool moms" of the priesthood. Also, he was in his mid-twenties and from Texas, so he wasn't just "cool" because he was a Gen X teacher; he also spoke with an Austin twang. And his daily uniform was cowboy boots and black Wrangler jeans, along with his clergy shirt collar.

Two years before I was first seated in Mr. Collins's classroom, *The Sopranos* was my jam, and having been raised on daytime soap operas and the interior lives of complicated women, I was always fascinated by Carmela Soprano. Which, according to writers ranging from James Baldwin to Hilton Als to Michael R. Jackson, a fascination with complicated white women in the media is most Black queer writers' first foray into cultural critique. That lends itself to an interest in icy blondes, from Barbara Stanwyck's Phyllis Dietrichson in *Double Indemnity* to Alison Sweeney's Sami Brady on *Days of Our Lives* back to Edie Falco's Carmela. The mob shit and all the sex scenes were fun for a teenager to watch on HBO, sure, but I was most interested in Tony Soprano's wife and her gauche new-money attire, perfectly coiffed bob, and the general nonchalance she applied to her life as a mob wife.

One of the best episodes of *The Sopranos* is season one's

"College," where Tony takes his daughter, Meadow, on a college tour and runs into a former snitch who is now in witness protection. It's a beautifully written episode about how the horrors of Tony's life are not just confined to his home but are also far-reaching and will linger wherever his children attempt to escape from him. The subplot in the episode involves Carmela falling ill and being visited by her priest, Father Phil. The two come dangerously close to kissing yet never do. But with the electricity in their scenes—and the extent to which every interaction was dripping with more tension than the moment Walter Neff witnesses Phyllis's ankle bracelet and honeysuckle scent of murder in *Double Indemnity* and becomes obsessively hooked—it became one of the series' most memorable episodes to me.

And then flash forward two years later, and here I was, sitting in English, reading Mark Twain and feeling like Carmela, lusting over my incredibly sexy English teacher with the Texas twang and cowboy boots. To my dismay at the time, we did not have a torrid affair in high school, and it did not become a *May December* situation. This would've been a completely different book. But he did encourage me in the way that the best English teachers do. Thanks to my previous year's obsession with Shakespeare, once we took on *Othello*, I got to lead the class in a group discussion for a week and learn how much I enjoy performing, despite never having the chance to do it in an actual school production.

Maybe there was some merit to being the villain in other people's high school stories. Because the power bestowed on me as one of Mr. Collins's favorite students turned me into the Regina George of English class. To this day, I am a perpetually late person, and I can directly trace this back to high school. I had to take two buses to school each morning—the 66 bus on the corner of 68th and Burleigh, then transfer to the 30 bus at Sherman and Burleigh, which would drop me off directly in front of school. But if I were to make my transfer, I had to turn off the television before the morning's syndicated rerun of *Beverly Hills, 90210* finished airing on Soapnet. Mr. Collins allowed my lateness, which pissed off the rest of my class. Because I cannot do anything without fully committing to a bit, I would also arrive with an iced coffee from Starbucks and a copy of the *Journal Sentinel*. Anything for a memorable entrance.

There was a brief period when I was on time—I didn't care much for *90210* once we got to season ten and Valerie Malone left the series. Gina Kincaid was a poor substitute for Valerie, and Vanessa Marcil should've stayed on *General Hospital* where she belonged! But once I discovered USA was airing reruns of *Charmed* in the same time slot, it was pretty much a wrap for me being on time to class.

Aside from being late, another way I pissed off my white classmates was ignoring their pleas to skip over the N-word while reading *Adventures of Huckleberry Finn* because it made them uncomfortable. What made me uncomfortable were the gay jokes I had endured from most of them since freshman year, so I relished the opportunity to make my classmates uncomfortable at any opportunity. I volunteered to read every day of the month of *Huckleberry Finn* and put some extra sauce on it when I read aloud the name "Nigger Jim." In 2011, a new U.S. edition of Twain's book was released that removed the more-than-two-hundred times the word "nigger" is written in *Huckleberry Finn*. Personally, I think censorship is out of control in America.

·   ·   ·

Like most American millennials, I spent most of my time not in school but at the mall. But let me stop you before you conjure up an image of me and my friends hanging out in the food court and shopping all afternoon like Cher and Dionne in *Clueless*. Most of my time at the mall was spent . . . reading.

I practically lived at Barnes & Noble at the Mayfair Mall, and it's no wonder that I would go on to work at that store after undergrad in New York and later in Los Angeles. The library was too far a bus ride and had an old smell and felt too much like a crypt. Meanwhile, Barnes & Noble had a faux Starbucks, brand-new books that I could read and then put back on the shelf, and glossy magazines. I could spend the day reading the latest issue of my favorite magazine, *Entertainment Weekly*, cover to cover, even though I already had a subscription. I usually read each issue more than once. In *Legally Blonde*, Elle Woods refers to *Cosmopolitan* magazine as the Bible, but to people who remember quotes from early-aughts movies like that, pop-culture obsessives who've gone on to make their career hosting podcasts and living out their adolescent fantasies of being a commentator on VH1's *Best Week Ever*, *Entertainment Weekly* was the Bible.

Entertainment Weekly covers were the height of my pop-culture obsession. They weren't high fashion—no one would ever accuse Annie Leibovitz of moonlighting for the magazine in between *Vogue* and *Vanity Fair* shoots—but they were *fun* and elevated the TV and movies I consumed to pop art, like with the cast of *Seinfeld*'s Beatles-inspired cover, Sarah Michelle Gellar's sexy cover wearing a tank top that said "Vampires Suck" on it, and the Dixie Chicks breaking their silence on their country-music ban after criticizing Bush with words like "traitors," "boycott," "hero," "free speech," and most hilariously, "Saddam's

angels" written on their bodies in black paint. Who needs Susan
Sontag's "Notes on 'Camp'" when *Entertainment Weekly* could
deliver camp like that to my door every week?

My second-favorite magazine was *Details*. A now-defunct
men's magazine published by Condé Nast, it was the only magazine besides *Entertainment Weekly* that I could see myself
working at. It was described as a "downtown" magazine in
comparison with the *Mad Men* vibes of *GQ*. This was when *GQ*
was marketed to men who owned three-piece suits, not the hip-
hop-listening sneakerheads who read it now. Mostly, *Details* was
just a really *gay* magazine. The covers were photos of hot male
celebrities and seemed more invested in making a reader horny
than being aspirational like the covers of *Men's Health*.

Before I was gay, I was a reader of *Details*, so maybe there is
something about the whole nature-versus-nurture thing in de-
termining sexuality. It was a choice to read *Details* from cover
to cover, and even if I didn't particularly care about the content
of each article I consumed, I could still tell that they were being
written by someone who was a real bitch. Since *Details* was a
gay magazine that masqueraded as a straight men's magazine,
it was perfectly safe for me to read in the bookstore while
downing a vanilla bean Frappuccino and some panini with
melted cheese. But as I mentioned before, this was a gateway
drug, and reading a magazine with hot men on the cover would
eventually cause my eyes to linger to the forbidden section of
Barnes & Noble as a closeted teenager: the Gay & Lesbian section, where magazines like *The Advocate*, *Out*, or *Instinct* had
men on covers that were very blatant about being horny-
inducing.

Those magazines I couldn't read in the café, and I certainly
couldn't buy them either, because somehow all closeted teenagers are trained to be ashamed of their purchases no matter

what store they're in. When I rushed to Sam Goody, a lost arti-
fact of the 2000s, a store where you would actually buy CDs in
person instead of listening to them on your phone, and purchased *NSYNC's third album, *No Strings Attached*, the morning it was released (contributing to its massive sales and record
of being the first album to sell over two million copies in one
week since SoundScan started recording data in 1991), I also
bought Ghostface Killah and Bone Thugs-N-Harmony albums
to hide my boy band purchase. And while Gran listened to gos-
pel music on Sunday mornings, I started my own praise-and-
worship sessions by listening to JC Chasez's soulful voice on "It
Makes Me Ill."

Since I wasn't going to purchase *Instinct* magazine and out
myself at my after-school and weekend haven, I had to devise
another option—theft. I stole gay magazines from Barnes &
Noble and read them in my bedroom with the door locked.
That tradition continued until I came out in the spring of 2005.

The tribe has spoken.

—JEFF PROBST, *SURVIVOR* (2000–PRESENT)

· · · · ·

THE WINNER TAKES IT ALL

ABBA and *Survivor* have two things in common.

One is they comfortably exist in the pop-culture category of things that were once and still are globally, immensely popular that have been kept alive by a rather large gay cult following. ABBA is indisputably one of the best bands to ever exist. If you wanted to show aliens pop music at its purest, most unadulterated form, you would play *ABBA Gold* for them, because it's famously the only ABBA album that most Americans own, as evidenced by the blank stares whenever I tell people my favorite ABBA song is "If It Wasn't for the Nights"* from their 1979 album *Voulez-Vouz*. The follow-up remark is invariably "Wait, *Voulez-Vouz* is an album? I thought it was a song."

And of course, straight people do love ABBA songs. Try escaping a straight (white) wedding without hearing "Dancing Queen." But it is gay people who keep the spirit of ABBA alive on the dance floor. "Gimme! Gimme! Gimme!" is about staying at the club just a little bit too long because you're horny and need to find a man to fuck, which, not surprisingly, made it a gay dance floor anthem later sampled by Madonna for her 2005

---

* A song about trying not to think about a man, but the literal act of the sun setting at night puts you in heat. The same can be said about "Out Tonight" from the musical *Rent*.

single "Hung Up." Oddly enough, "Gimme! Gimme! Gimme!" seems to have been phased out of most recent dance floors, at least in New York, the only city that matters, and replaced with "Voulez-Vous." They're essentially the same song, but the latter is more gender-fluid.*

The second thing ABBA and *Survivor* have in common is that both value the art of war. It's odd to think of ABBA as warmongers, but their best songs are literally about the competitive nature of love. "Gimme! Gimme! Gimme!" and "Voulez-Vous" are about winning a man on the dance floor. Using Napoleon as a metaphor, the song "Waterloo" is about realizing you should settle for someone if they're in love with you. "The Winner Takes It All" has the theme of the song in the title. One thing about winners? They get everything. And more than anything, people love to win. Which brings us to American elections.

And why the year 2004 was the most intense of my life as a voter. No, not because of George fucking Bush. Because of *American Idol* season three.

On April 28, 2004, I witnessed the real face of racism in America when my votes failed to keep Jennifer Hudson, LaToya London, and Fantasia Barrino from being in the bottom three on *American Idol* during Barry Manilow week. Back in 2004, people gave a shit about *American Idol*. The series, which debuted in the fall of 2000, was still hosted by the original trio of Simon Cowell (a British asshole who wore tight black V-necked shirts), Paula Abdul (then considered a washed-up eighties/nineties pop star who used the show to claw her way back to fame and also remind bitches that she used to choreograph for Janet Jackson, so you *will* fucking respect her), and Randy Jack-

---

* Obviously, "Dancing Queen" is also a gay anthem, but much like "I Love Rock 'n' Roll," sexy songs about seventeen-year-olds weird me out.

son (the worst judge on the show, but maybe I'm biased because before I got LASIK, people actually used to mistake me for him all the time).

Ryan Seacrest, a literal Ken doll (not sure he's actually anatomic), was the perennially upbeat emcee of the series. The reality show was ostensibly about the hunt for the best singer in America, but it was also inspired by many similar series that had come before it, like *Star Search*.

Almost as important as the singing were the clip packages attached to each contestant. Before auditioning, singers would share their (traumatic) life stories and what brought them to the show. As the show continued to be a ratings success (its season-two finale garnered 38.1 million people to watch Ruben Studdard beat Clay Aiken), the stories got even more traumatic. What started with "I used to sleep in my car while playing guitar at a coffee shop on the weekends" turned into "my mother shot herself in the head while I watched."

Barring Studdard's win, the series' first few seasons managed to produce actual superstar winners. Kelly Clarkson won the first season. Fantasia Barrino won the third. Carrie Underwood won the fourth. The fifth season saw Katharine McPhee lose tragically to Taylor Hicks, but in retrospect, after being inflicted with her acting on *Smash* and discovering the revelation that she pandered to gay men on the internet for relevance while secretly voting Republican, I'm now perfectly fine with her losing! Jordin Sparks won the sixth season, and while millennials fondly remember her and the single "No Air," she marked the beginning of the end of *American Idol* producing massive stars. Every subsequent winner is mainly remembered for *winning American Idol*, not because of any success after the series.

During the actual competition, a bunch of singers would get a ticket to Hollywood, where they'd go through a hell week of competition that would bring us to our top-twelve finalists, who would then go on to compete until a winner was crowned. Each week, the competition would have normal themes like country, Elton John, and Motown. There would also be Barry Manilow to draw in older audiences and familiarize millennial teenagers with sixties pop songs they would've never heard otherwise. *American Idol* was the original TikTok.

Then there was the Jigsaw-from-*Saw* of a theme called disco week, where no single person ever sounded good except for Kimberley Locke when she sang "It's Raining Men" in season two. Sometimes when I go to bed at night I'm still haunted by the sounds of Carmen Rasmusen fighting her way through a rendition of "Turn the Beat Around" in the same season.

But back to that week in April 2004—the top six compete. Diana DeGarmo kicks off the evening by singing "One Voice," a non-single track from the 1979 Manilow album *One Voice*. At times, the song threatens to be sexy in the way the Bee Gees could make easy listening sound like something you'd want to fuck to, but for the most part, it's just as boring as Diana's performance. Diana is the doe-eyed white girl of the season (every season has at least one!). She is a sixteen-year-old from Snellville, Georgia, who speaks formally by addressing Simon Cowell as "Mr. Simon." Diana is who Fox wanted Americans to tune in for and vote for, so the judges' critiques are restrained. But Diana had been in the bottom three for the past two weeks, so in response to this performance, Simon offers up: "Without question, your best performance in the entire competition." He doesn't clarify whether that means the performance was *good*, but he doesn't need to! He says enough that people won't call him mean for attacking a sweet white girl on TV, and he also doesn't have to lie and say he liked it.

George Huff is next: a twenty-three-year-old from New

Orleans who sounds like my Marlboro-chain-smoking great-grandfather when he speaks and like Luther Vandross if he couldn't quite get the right key when he sings. He performs "Tryin' to Get the Feeling Again." First sung by the Carpenters in 1975, it's the best version of this song, but it wasn't released until 1994 because at the time they had too many ballads on their sixth album, *Horizon*. It became a hit for Manilow in 1976. The judges hated it, as you can tell from the "nice" judge, Paula, stumbling her way through a compliment. "You stayed in time with the music" is such a wild thing to offer to a singer, because isn't that the entire point?

Jennifer Hudson goes third, singing Manilow's 1976 single "Weekend in New England." It's a gorgeous performance, and Jennifer does what she does best: puts the proper emphasis on words in a song to really drive it home. And there's a run in the song that makes you want to leap out of your chair. She took *American Idol* all the way to church and sang the fucking auditorium down, which is more than the show deserved.

Jasmine Trias is next, and in case you did not know she is from Hawaii, she wears a flower in her hair every week. First, she is done the incredibly rude disservice of having to stand there while Ryan introduces the cast of the new Fox reality series *The Swan*, a show about women getting plastic surgery to get a man (relatable, TBH). Then she performs "I'll Never Love This Way Again," a Dionne Warwick song that Barry produced, and it's a beautiful rendition. No notes. Another recurring theme of *American Idol* is that the women are always great, and the men, much like Barbie's boyfriend, Ken, are just there.

LaToya London follows that performance by singing "All the Time" from Barry's 1976 album *This One's for You*. It's a great performance, and LaToya adds a lot of sauce to an otherwise-forgettable song. She's the second-best of the night so far, and you know the DeGarmo stans were at home furiously tying up the phone lines so no one could vote for her.

John Stevens, a sixteen-year-old white boy from Upstate New York who seemed like he would grow up to become a serial killer (but didn't, as far as I know . . .), was oddly very endearing on the show. He didn't have iconic performances, but he had a lovely voice, and you always wanted to give him a hug and say, "Good job!" after he sang. Well, until he mangles "Mandy" onstage like a drunk in a karaoke bar. Randy and Simon are the only ones who give the performance a bad critique, which isn't shocking, but what is shocking are the unhinged comments on a YouTube video of John's performance. One person goes as far as to claim that John Stevens is the only *American Idol* contestant they remember, and I am quickly reminded that not only was the voting on *American Idol* racist, but like most voters in America, the majority of people voting for it were deeply stupid.

Fantasia wraps up the week by doing "It's a Miracle," which, unfortunately, is her only bad performance in the entire series. But in her defense, it is not a good song. It's one of those uptempo songs where the vocals sound mostly like talking and don't show off anyone's singing prowess, least of all Barry's, so it's no surprise it did no favors for Fantasia either.

The next night, Fantasia lands in the bottom three, which is fine! Landing in the bottom at least once builds a winning narrative on a reality competition show—the audience needs to fear for your safety and vote even harder the next week. But the absolute best performers of the night are in the bottom alongside her. But *American Idol* doles out the news that all three Black women are in the bottom in the cruelest way possible. The women are separated into Group A, while Diana, Jasmine, and John are put into Group B. George is told he's safe, and then Ryan asks him to join the top group onstage. Naturally, because he heard the singing last night like everyone else, he tries to join Group A—before Ryan reiterates, "The *top* group," almost gleefully enjoying it as he reveals to the audience that a shocking turn of events has just happened: One of the three best singers in the competition will be going home.

When Jennifer is eliminated, Fantasia gives her a big hug and shouts, "You are *my* American Idol." Jennifer's loss, of course, is no big deal in the grand scheme of things, because she has a damn Oscar. And Fantasia nearly going home galvanized voters to make sure it would never happen again, so they continued to vote for her every week until she won the competition over, you guessed it, America's Southern belle, Diana.

This episode pulled apart the entire conceit of *American Idol*. Winning *American Idol* would turn out to mean absolutely nothing because the best singers were often eliminated by chance and would still go on to have massive careers despite not winning the grand prize.* *American Idol* in its original incarnation ran for fifteen seasons, before it was taken off the air and then revived by ABC and in recent seasons hosted by Keith Urban, Katy Perry, and Lionel Richie. It is one of the most inessential shows on TV, and the only time it was relevant in any cultural conversation was when Katy struggled to understand what a gay contestant meant by saying the word "wig."†

. . .

---

* Maybe the most psychotic thing about *American Idol* is that when you get eliminated, you have to sing the song that got you eliminated one more time. Like, babe, America already said no thanks!

† As in "You snatched my wig." As in "I'm shocked, in disbelief."

In contrast, the reality competition series *Survivor*, which also debuted in the early 2000s, is still on the air but is a much more culturally relevant series. There are many reasons for this. One, it manages to remain shocking and entertaining twenty-four years on. Two, gay people watch it. Ratings-wise, *American Idol* and *Survivor* are pretty much on par with each other, but no one is tweeting about *American Idol* week to week like they do for *Survivor*. The ABC run of *American Idol* has produced seven winners so far—Maddie Poppe, Laine Hardy, Just Sam (let's workshop that name), Chayce Beckham, Noah Thompson, Iam Tongi, and Abi Carter. I am not being hyperbolic when I say I have never heard of any of these people before. And two of them are male country singers, which just *feels* homophobic.

Twenty-four years after its debut, *Survivor* has still managed to be a watercooler TV show season after season. Fans analyze the gameplay, the casting department still manages to cast people who are entertaining to watch, and most important, they put a lot of hot men (until recently, but thank God for *Australian Survivor*, where even the nerds are smoking hot and six feet tall and have eight-pack abs, and the reigning gay on the series, self-dubbed King George, is an absolutely cocky bitch who is so much fun to watch) and dynamic women on a beach to compete for a million dollars, which is basically a gay fever dream. Former contestants even compete on the extremely popular new Peacock series *The Traitors*, where they play against other reality stars.

Hosted by aging carnival barker Jeff Probst, a collection of castaways hits the beach and is split into tribes before having to build a camp, start a fire, and compete in immunity challenges. The rules of *Survivor* are to "outwit, outplay, and outlast," but the beauty of the game is that despite the athletic prowess often required to win challenges, it is very rare that a challenge beast (a name coined by fans of the series in online forums) wins the big prize at the end.

Fans and soon other players in the game began to refer to people who racked up multiple individual immunity-challenge wins (individual immunity is awarded once the tribes merge into one tribe midseason) in a season—like Rob "Boston Rob" Mariano, Ozzy Lusth, Kim Spradlin, Tyson Apostol, Joe Anglim, and Spencer Bledsoe—as challenge beasts. But in the forty-six seasons of *Survivor* that have aired so far, most of the winners haven't been so-called challenge beasts. More often than not, castaways will start to pick off the strong men and the challenge beasts to ensure that everyone else has a fighting chance at winning. The best to ever play the game, Sandra Diaz-Twine (so good she crossed over to *Australian Survivor*, but it was a nothing appearance, since she went out pre-merge), routinely sat out of challenges when she could. Yet she's managed to win the game twice. Richard Hatch, the villainous gay who won the first-ever season of *Survivor*, only won immunity once during his season.

The *Survivor* fan base tends to love people who make big, strategic moves, blindside their opponents with surprise maneuvers, and are generally *smart*. For as much as the show still has the reputation that it's basically *Fear Factor*, a 2000s NBC series where people had to eat bugs and shit to win, *Survivor* abandoned more of the grosser elements (like eating cow brains and worms) as the series went on. Some of *Survivor's* most renowned players—Cirie Fields (winner of *The Traitors* season one), Parvati Shallow (great at challenges), Yul Kwon, and John Cochran (also great at challenges)—are really just brilliant at strategy and reading their opponents' emotions.

It's no wonder, then, that the series has such a gay fan base. Not that I would count out gays in a fight of brute strength and endurance, but stereotypically we've had to outwit, outplay, and outlast to survive, and watching the brawny jocks get taken out by calculating men and women who use not only their brains to triumph, but also their social skills, is a great thing to live vicariously through.

At the height of the series' popularity, *Survivor: All-Stars* debuted after Super Bowl XXXVIII (otherwise known as the infamous Janet Jackson and Justin Timberlake wardrobe-malfunction performance), and my friends were absolutely obsessed with it. Most kids who grow up watching *Survivor* have always wanted to be *on* it, but I already knew I had no chance of competing. First, I can't swim.

I drowned in Denmark in the fourth grade. Not Jack-in-*Titanic* drowned, but more of everything went black, and then I woke up on the side of the pool after going under. I attended Golda Meir for elementary school, a public school for "gifted and talented" kids. I had a teacher, Mr. Horowitz, who taught us Danish in preparation for a two-week trip to Denmark and the Netherlands to study the history of World War II. Amsterdam has become one of my favorite places to travel as an adult, but I have yet to return to Copenhagen, the site of my first nemesis.

We stayed with a host family with a son named Henrik who was in my grade. Henrik and I hated each other from the moment we met, mostly because I was still incredibly antisocial and spent most of my time reading and not trying to make friends. As an adult who likes to travel, spending time alone drinking and reading and smoking cigarettes is how I want to enjoy my vacation. But in fourth grade, on this class trip, I was forced to interact daily with someone who kept humming Oasis every five seconds. To this day, even hearing "Wonderwall" sends me into a rage (Liam Gallagher and I have that in common, at least). I don't blame myself entirely. Henrik was also evil Macaulay Culkin from *The Good Son*. He delighted in tormenting me when adults weren't around.

On one occasion, while swimming at one of the public pools in Copenhagen, our bubbling animosity brewed into a brawl that left me with a bloody nose and submerged in the water. What followed was a *Jaws*-level fear of swimming. And then, as my body changed from that of a scrawny nerd who could get beaten up by a goddamn Scandinavian (I should've taken this to the grave) to an even nerdier fat kid, I had even less desire to learn how to swim and expose my body to my friends and classmates.

But I *was* smart. If I couldn't outplay, then I could outwit on *Survivor*. The show itself leaned hard into the dichotomy with two seasons subtitled *Brawn vs. Brains vs. Beauty* (only the first season was good). The seasons were critiqued for dividing people into a "beauty" tribe, but listen, one thing millennials grew up learning was that some people are hot, and some people are not. If you're not hot, you should be funny or smart. This was also the basic premise of ABC's reality competition series *Are You Hot?*, where former soap opera star Lorenzo Lamas pointed a red laser at contestants' near-naked bodies to highlight their imperfections. Hot people were on the show. Non-hot, funny people wrote hilariously scathing reviews of the show. Everyone wins.

My high school did not have the typical archetypes of a coed school, but we were evenly divided by nerd and jock (rich kids could be either). Not in a way that nerds were preyed upon by the jocks like in an eighties teen comedy, but jocks tended to work out together in the morning and care about winning games and listening to rap music. The nerds tended to like art class and do theater and listen to rock music. I had friends in both groups, which is why I know I am perfectly suited to win the game of *Survivor* even though I will never apply for it because I am not trying to live on a desert island.

But at Marquette, where social groups were much more fluid than at a regular high school (one of the only TV shows to actually get this was *Beverly Hills, 90210*, where very hot Kelly Taylor and Steve Sanders hung out with losers Brandon and Brenda Walsh and also drug addict Dylan McKay, because the one thing they all had in common was being rich), I befriended both sides of the aisle. Most of the time, I would eat lunch with the art kids, but I liked going to the jocks' parties because they did not eventually devolve into listening to underground Milwaukee punk music that was mostly a lot of screaming.

The other thing about *Survivor* obsessives is that they have once in their life *played* the game. Not the official game, but they've managed to gather a bunch of friends over a weekend to play a mock version of the game. Not content with that, I convinced my friends to play *Survivor* at our lunch table. There were around fifteen of us general regulars at the table, most of them art kids, but a couple of them were floaters like me or jocks who also did theater or liked to paint, which is giving *Glee*, but *Glee* wasn't out yet, which is another reason why most millennial kids waited until college to come out of the closet.

We didn't have singing and dancing gays and allies on our TV screens every week; we had whiny Jack McPhee (on a show with Dawson Leery, TV's most annoying character ever, mind you, and a reason to make you never want to attend film school) on *Dawson's Creek*, who cured the town's homophobia by joining the football team.

The game version of *Survivor* we devised involved voting out a different person from the lunch table each day until there was only one person left. In retrospect this was a very bad idea, because it revealed itself to mostly be a popularity contest and a quick revelation of which people we tolerated hanging out with at lunch who we didn't particularly like. It was a social, active form of bullying, but then again, *Survivor* in and of itself is a popularity contest too.

The other thing about high school students, however, is that we get tired of things very easily, so we decided to crown a winner when there were six of us left. I did not win, because as I said, *Survivor* and high school are popularity contests, but *Survivor* is also a game where you can beat the odds by amassing an alliance or winning a hidden immunity idol. And Stephen, a person who most of my friends didn't particularly care for, had a basement where everyone hung out most nights after school and on weekends, so of course he had to be voted the winner, because where else were we gonna hang out?

The third and most important voting day of my life occurred on November 2, 2004. The first year I was eligible to vote, I registered in the summer between high school ending and college beginning. Having gone to school with the kids of Republicans who let them affix Bush–Cheney stickers to their cars the entire first four years of the George W. Bush administration, I had never been more excited than I was to vote for John Kerry.

As we geared up for the general election, most of my friends had Kerry stickers on their cars, and the ones who didn't, whose parents probably did vote for Bush, had the good sense to not parade it around. Politics in Milwaukee in 2003 seemed very *quiet* to me, particularly because I had been sent to a school where talking about politics was not something you were supposed to do.

It wasn't until college, when I joined the school's theater department, that I was introduced to the vigor that came with student politics. Student politics until then involved the brats who ran student government, not students who literally registered people to vote on campus and also campaigned for their preferred candidate as fiercely as they learned a monologue to audition for *A Midsummer Night's Dream*.

I didn't return home for Election Day, so I voted absentee and went with my friends to my very first Election Night party. Everyone there was rooting for Kerry except for the one straight asshole in the theater department. Straight men in a theater department wield far too much power, unfortunately, because the women *and* the gays are attracted to them. I shouldn't have later been shocked that this Bush supporter would enjoy putting a little *too* much emphasis on the word "nigger" when we read *Ma Rainey's Black Bottom* in class. When it was clear Bush was winning a second term and that Kerry would be conceding that next day, I witnessed everyone around me except him sobbing. Not the crying that came from liberals the night Trump won; that was more shell shock. This was crying because we had been assured victory at first, only to have it snatched away from us.

The whole stolen-election nonsense from Trump might seem new to you if you didn't experience the 2004 election firsthand, but there was a voter-fraud conspiracy theory that popped up in 2004 after Bush won his second term. Most people tended to agree that Bush stole his first election, or rather, the Supreme Court handed it to him. There was a recount underway after Al Gore's loss to Bush in 2000, and most newspapers at the time agreed that if the recount of disputed Florida votes had been done, then Gore would've won by a narrow margin. According to a 2001 *New York Times* article, "If all the ballots had been reviewed under any of seven single standards and combined with the results of an examination of overvotes,

Mr. Gore would have won, by a very narrow margin. For example, using the most permissive 'dimpled chad' standard, nearly 25,000 additional votes would have been reaped, yielding 644 net new votes for Mr. Gore and giving him a 107-vote victory margin."

The Supreme Court decided that it'd be better to just ignore those results and hand the election to Bush. Since then, conservatives and the Supreme Court have used this tactic to decide whatever they want to be law, basically. Like stripping away abortion rights in 2022. All because they have a majority in the Supreme Court.

These conspiracies and the chipping-away of Supreme Court norms are what, like *American Idol*, made the presidency all but obsolete in the minds of voters and the people running the country. Because if the winner doesn't have the power to stop a Supreme Court from doing wildly flagrant shit, then what's the point of the competition in the first place? And it makes you feel like one of Obama's pull toy phrases, originally from Martin Luther King, Jr., "The arc of the moral universe is long, but it bends towards justice," feel as empty as a reality TV singing-competition vote.

But it *is* a true statement, not because the world bends toward justice on its own, but because it is quite literally dragged there. It requires action, not inaction. It's why the presidency is a lot like *American Idol*. There's not a lot of *action* occurring. Sure, you can campaign for votes. Sure, America will vote for their candidate, and if America has good taste, the right person will win, like Barack Obama or Kelly Clarkson or Fantasia Barrino. But Americans are not smart, I must remind you, so you must always treat life as a competition like *Survivor* and not *American Idol*. In *Survivor*, the winner plots, schemes, finds hidden immunity idols, amasses alliances, and can sometimes even be voted out and return to the game. Like Chris Underwood, who infamously won season thirty-eight of *Survivor: Edge of Extinction* after being voted out on day eight, and returned to the game only to cruise to victory against Gavin Whitson and Julie Rosenberg. In a season of absurd twists, he still managed to prevail, and though he might be hated by most *Survivor* fans, he still *won*.

When I think of who exudes the most "winner takes it all" energy, I think of Theresa Lopez-Fitzgerald.

On July 5, 1999, millennials at home watching *Days of Our Lives* with their parents were introduced to the campy supernatural soap *Passions*, created by James E. Reilly. NBC gave Reilly carte blanche to create a new soap opera after he did the impossible of raising *Days'* ratings while it aired alongside the O. J. Simpson trial. He did so by writing a storyline where one of the show's heroines, Dr. Marlena Evans (still played to this day by Deidre Hall), was possessed by the devil in 1995. From the success of that plot, Reilly created a series where most of the storylines were supernatural. And millennials ate it up.

One of my favorite scenes in cinema is Elle Woods in *Legally Blonde* describing *Days of Our Lives* plotlines in her Harvard submission: "Once again, we join Hope in the search for her identity. As you know, she's been brainwashed by the evil Stefano." This is exactly how my classmates and I sounded when we discussed *Passions* during lunch: how Charity Standish was frozen in a block of ice while her wicked cousin Kay Bennett and a zombie version of Charity, rather straightforwardly named Zombie Charity, terrorized the town of Harmony by opening the door to hell via a closet. And there was a witch named Tabitha and a talking doll named Timmy (portrayed by Josh Ryan Evans, who had achondroplasia, which left him with the appearance and voice of a child at age twenty. In a very weird turn of events, his character, who was set to die and become an angel permanently on the show, died in the August 5, 2002, episode, the same day Evans himself died from heart complications).

But the standout character in *Passions* is Theresa Lopez-Fitzgerald. Played by Lindsay Hartley from the series' debut till its finale in 2008, she is the glue that holds the series together. A mix of heroine and antiheroine, she is in love with Ethan Crane, the son of the incredibly wealthy and evil Julian Crane. Infatuated with him from the moment we meet her, she manages to steal him away from the scheming, rich blonde Gwen Hotchkiss. Ethan and Theresa become engaged and have sex, and unbeknownst to them, she becomes pregnant. Gwen and her mother, Rebecca Hotchkiss, discover that Ethan is not actually Julian's son and that his mother, Ivy, had had an affair with Sam Bennett, the town sheriff. Acting out of jealousy, Gwen and and her mother send this information to the tabloids from Theresa's computer, setting her up and making Ethan and Ivy think she'd destroyed his life for a quick buck. Julian disowns Ethan, and Theresa flies to Bermuda to plead with him to adopt Ethan, but after getting drunk with Julian, she sleeps with him, marries him, and then is led to believe the child she is carrying is Julian's. She spends the next six years trying to win Ethan back and prove her innocence.

Theresa sweeps through multiple marriages over the course of the series' nine-year run, a true soap diva in the vein of Susan Lucci's legendary Erica Kane. But there is more to Theresa's story than merely being a girl looking for love in all the wrong places. Theresa is Latina, and being in love with the handsome white heir to a family fortune forever made her a target. Season after season, she is never able to forget that she was born to the maid of the richest family in Harmony and that her skin is darker than everyone else's around her.

Other characters taunt Theresa with insults like "Terrorcita," "Enchilada," and every other item on the Taco Bell menu. Their cruelty may seem over-the-top, but their behavior mimics the far-too-real ways actual people use "joking racism" to continually put nonwhite people down and certainly mirrors most of the "funny" race jokes that got told to me at Marquette. I didn't have the power to punch one student in the face for making a lynching joke in front of me, lest I wanted to be kicked out of school, but every day I could go home and watch Theresa fighting endlessly to triumph over her adversaries, and being closeted at Marquette felt a lot like sprawling, unrequited soap opera love when you had a crush on someone and feared anyone at all finding out.

When Theresa is accused of murdering Julian Crane, the wealthiest man in Harmony, the racist and patriarchal machinations of the Harmony caste system mean a death sentence for her when she is ultimately tried and convicted. But goddamn, that bitch manages to survive a *lethal injection*. When she is given the injection, she doesn't die—her heart merely slows to an unrecognizable frequency. Even after her enemies crow over her body at her wake and plunge a letter opener into her heart, she isn't killed. The body in that casket isn't Theresa's after all, having long since been replaced with a wax replica. As insane a plot twist as this is, the gay little tears that welled in my eyes during Theresa's almost-death scene were very real.

Theresa would eventually prove that she did not shoot Julian (and that he was still alive) and that she did not send the information about Ethan's paternity to the tabloids. In one of the most hilarious scenes that has ever been on TV, Theresa hunts down J. T. Cornell, the sleazy reporter who Gwen had sold Ethan's paternity secret to.

What you need to know about soap operas is that because they're on every day, most viewers dip in and out and return after missing stretches of episodes. (*Days* tried to combat this with the tagline "Miss a *Days*, miss a lot!" It was very much not true; Marlena was again possessed by the devil in 2021, and she's been fighting her own blond rival, Kristen DiMera, since the nineties.) Soaps *love* exposition. Exposition dumps happen every day and start to feel like you're hearing your best friend tell the same story they love to tell at parties for the hundredth time. But on *Passions*, the exposition is taken to an extreme.

While racing through the streets of Rome looking for J. T., who is also being chased by Gwen, Theresa pauses to let viewers know why she is running after him: "Gwen! She's after J. T.! She probably wants to get the proof that he has, that she and her mother sent the information to the tabloid revealing Ethan's true paternity, before J. T. has a chance to show it to Ethan. But I've gotta get the truth so Ethan'll believe that I'm telling the truth that Gwen was actually the one who betrayed him . . . Maybe Ethan will realize that everything I did, I did because I love him."

All the things she did? Stalking; breaking and entering; attacking a wheelchair-using Ivy with a fire poker; plotting murder; blackmailing; chloroforming and knocking out Ethan and Gwen's surrogate to take her place so she could force them to give custody of her son to her in exchange for their baby; and countless other schemes. And after all of that, in the final episode of *Passions*, when Theresa is vindicated . . . she and Ethan get married. And she wins everything. Because if the end is right, then it justifies the schemes.

How *Sex and the City* are we right now? I'm Samantha, you're
Charlotte, and you're the lady at home who watches it.

—JENNA MARONEY, *30 ROCK* (2007)

· · · · ·

FAN FICTION

Because I'm a gay millennial, I've had to tell far too many
friends, "No, you are not a Carrie. And you're *certainly* not
a Samantha." Because of the easily recognizable archetypes of
Sex and the City, the main character (Sarah Jessica Parker's Carrie Bradshaw), the ethical ho (Kim Cattrall's Samantha Jones),
the businesswoman (Cynthia Nixon's Miranda Hobbes), and
the conservative (Kristin Davis's Charlotte York), viewers love
to assign one of these women to their own personality.

Because of the overwhelming narcissism of millennials,
most people consider themselves to be a Carrie. Most people
are not a Carrie. Yes, most people believe themselves to be the
leading lady in their own lives, moving from romance to heartbreak at every corner, but that doesn't make you Carrie; it just
means you've dated in your twenties and thirties. As excellent
TV critic and harrowing tweeter Emily Nussbaum wrote in her
New Yorker essay "Difficult Women," Carrie is an antihero.
Granted, Nussbaum does refer to Carrie as "the unacknowl-
edged *first* female anti-hero on TV," which ignores Susan Lucci's businesswoman/man-eater/bear fighter* Erica Kane on *All*

---

* If you haven't seen Erica Kane fight off a bear in a nineties episode of *All My
Children*, then google it immediately.

My Children or Heather Locklear's icy bitch/advertising exec/ slumlord Amanda Woodward on *Melrose Place*, but most television criticism tends to gloss over soaps.

To be a Carrie, you should probably be a writer prone to toxic romantic relationships and reckless decisions, like having affairs with married men or fleeing to Paris with a Russian you just met because you've always imagined a life in Europe smoking cigarettes, drinking wine, and shopping all day while putting off your deadlines. Most people are not Carries. They are Mirandas or Charlottes, people who have a lot of *rules* that prevent them from finding love but eventually meet the right person and all those rules are thrown out the window.

Very few people are sexually liberated enough to be a Samantha—most gay men, for instance, think they are Samanthas because the amount of sex that gay men have in comparison to heterosexual people statistically is comical. Which is why we don't participate in the heterosexual ritual of comparing "body counts," meaning the amount of people you've fucked in your lifetime. This is why you must factor in Samantha's business acumen and no-nonsense attitude, and that is where most aspiring Samanthas falter.

Personally, I know my traits as a romantic partner and the narcissist behavior that comes not only with being a Leo—and someone who tells people about their astrological sign at every chance they get—but also with having the gall to write little stories about my life and assume that they are of great importance. Toni Morrison did once say, "If there's a book that you want to read, but it hasn't been written yet, then you must write it," and who the hell else is writing a book about my life but me? I *must* be a Carrie.

But the main reason that I associate with Carrie Bradshaw is not merely because I am a writer, nor because I have a self-aggrandized inclination toward sharing my life with the world, but because I also *love* other people's business. Unlike most millennials, I did not watch *Sex and the City* in secret on HBO for the salacious sex scenes while also aspiring to live in Carrie's chic Manhattan apartment. I watched *Sex and the City* because Carrie was a columnist and I desperately wanted to be a writer living in New York.

The HBO series and Carrie's weekly sex column were based on self-proclaimed sexual anthropologist Candace Bushnell's real-life column "Sex and the City," which she wrote for *The New York Observer* from 1994 to 1996, then published in a book anthology of the same name. In a 2022 interview with Jia Tolentino for *The New Yorker*, Bushnell says she wanted to emulate Joan Didion and the staccato sentence structure of Joseph Heller. As a recovering English major, I've only ever read Heller's *Catch-22* ages ago, so I can't comment much on his sentence structure, but Bushnell did capture a certain spirit of Didion's writing in that her writing made it feel like New York City was living and breathing, much like Didion's did for California. Though it has been dismissed as "fluff," she was writing real stories about a certain set of New Yorkers' sex and social lives—it *was* anthropology.

It's also, frankly, why *Sex and the City* still works when you rewatch it. Even the episodes that seem dated and cringeworthy now, like when Samantha dates a Black guy in the season-three episode "No Ifs, Ands or Butts":

SAMANTHA: That is one fine-looking man. I'd like to get me some of that.
CHARLOTTE: Don't talk like that.
SAMANTHA: Like what?
CHARLOTTE: You know.

SAMANTHA: Oh, relax with the knee-jerk liberal reaction. That wasn't Black talk; that was sex talk.

CHARLOTTE: Okay, first of all, it isn't "Black talk." It's African American talk. And you shouldn't be talking like that at all, Samantha. It's rude and politically incorrect.

CARRIE: Sweetie, a reminder: Samantha *is* rude and politically incorrect.

MIRANDA: She's an equal opportunity offender.

SAMANTHA: Precisely. I don't see color; I see conquest.

For one thing, the exchange is fucking hysterical. It feels like the shit that society white women who rarely interacted with Black people would say in the year 2000 (because the writers were rich white people who rarely interacted with Black people). These are the same people who would describe the Meatpacking District in 2000 as "trendy by day, tranny by night," which is why Samantha *also* says that in the season-three episode "Cock-a-Doodle-Do." This season is the last that creator Darren Star worked on with Michael Patrick King, which is unfortunate, because it's one of the series' most emotionally rich, from having Carrie fuck Big behind her boyfriend Aidan's back to embracing topical stories like bisexuality, golden shower sexual fetishes, and New Yorkers realizing that their dream of moving to Los Angeles is actually a nightmare.

Bushnell's contemporaries were writers like Bret Easton Ellis and Jay McInerney, who similarly wrote romans à clef about their own lives in Los Angeles and New York City, respectively. Which is to say that all three writers wrote about their lives and the lives of their friends, family, and random strangers they encountered and added a little sauce to it to call it fiction. The knowledge that what you're reading is just

gossip, other people's business, makes it something more salacious and addictive. It's why the mostly superfluous novel *The
Devil Wears Prada* became such a megahit and a film, because
it was a thinly veiled account of Lauren Weisberger's tenure
as *Vogue* editor Anna Wintour's personal assistant.* And what
part of that wouldn't appeal to the generation that quite literally shared not only their innermost thoughts but also the private lives of their own friends and classmates on a little website
called LiveJournal in the early to mid-2000s?

Generations older than millennials might have been used to
writing in physical diaries—I know such things exist because
I've watched *The Notebook*—but teenagers of my generation
used to pour out their hearts on the internet, and not always
privately. These diary entries were for *other people to read*. Call it
self-obsessed or psychotic, but I used to write down how the
day and my friends used to make me feel.

The way I'm sure some of Bushnell's ex-lovers got mad
about her depicting them in her weekly column, I recall a teenage jealousy over my then–best friend spending most of his
time with his new girlfriend, so I wrote a journal entry about
how much I disliked her. That did *not* go over well, but I did
maintain friendships with both after a very tense summer, and
now they're each married to other people and probably don't
even remember the summer I wielded LiveJournal as a weapon
against their relationship.

---

* Unfortunately, the film's lasting legacy is quarterly debated on social media
as to who the "true villain" of the film is: Anne Hathaway's Andy Sachs, Meryl
Streep's Miranda Priestly, or Andy's boyfriend and friends. The true villain is
actual people with nothing better to do than keep beating to death the same
topic about a 2006 film. I realize the irony of me, writing a book about pop
culture, saying this, but it's maybe the most obnoxious crime committed by
pop-culture nostalgia media. And this is coming from someone who worked at
BuzzFeed when Netflix bought the rights to *Friends* in 2015.

Is it, then, any wonder that a generation who grew up on LiveJournal would in turn fall in love with the 2007 TV series *Gossip Girl*, which was all about an anonymous blogger spilling the tea on all their rich New York classmates? In a way, it's probably the reason the Max sequel series to *Gossip Girl* didn't really work and why at times *And Just Like That . . .* doesn't really work either—the central conceit of these series was *tea*.

On the reboot of *Gossip Girl*, you had teachers creepily monitoring their students' sex lives and blasting it to the internet. That's not tea; that's grounds for being on a sex offender list. Meanwhile, *And Just Like That . . .* does have the same sensibility as the original series in that it feels like Michael Patrick King is trying to figure out what's going on in the modern world and write about it by adding in a bunch of women of color and a nonbinary terrorist of a character named Che Diaz—but it feels like the *writers* are trying to figure out the modern world and not Carrie. Carrie is too busy grieving the death of Big to be all up in her friends' business, to wonder about what dating is like for a widow in New York City in the 2020s, or to figure out whether dating has changed for *younger* women in the city. She's entirely uncurious in the sequel series, and who really wants to call themselves a Carrie when she's not a nosy bitch anymore?

By 2002, I was watching *Passions* daily. That, coupled with my obsession with spilling my innermost thoughts on the internet, led me to write a fictional soap opera named *Guasti Cose* and publish it on the internet. Essentially creating my own version of *Passions* and *Days of Our Lives*, I spent my time writing about a family in Wisconsin that was plagued with affairs, scandals, and demons attempting to pull the world into hell.

My favorite class of course became computer science, because it was one of three hours (the second was lunch, the third my free period) where I had unfettered access to the internet without having to negotiate online time with my grandmother—we still had an AOL dial-up, and using the internet tied up the phone line, which meant my nighttime internet usage was very limited until we got a second phone line.

I published episodes often, and I felt comfortable admitting to some of my friends that I was writing a sometimes daily, sometimes weekly soap opera for strangers to read on an internet forum called EpiGuide that was run by one of my first writing mentors, a woman who I've never met named Kira Lerner (all I know about her is that she loved cats and lived in New York City but maybe also never left her apartment). I became friends with many strangers who shared a love of daytime and prime-time soap operas and writing.

More than any class I've ever had on writing, it was writing *Guasti Cose* every chance I got that sated my aspirations of having people read my writing. Every time I churned out an episode, I would impatiently wait for someone to comment in the series' forum, leaving praise or critiques of the episode. It was the critiques that made me first learn how to handle real-life criticism of my writing. At first, there was the ego sting of realizing something I'd written wasn't perfect—I still have this problem twenty years later!—but then the realization that people I didn't even personally know were somehow invested enough in what I was writing to bother commenting on it made me suck it up and learn how to be a better writer.

I met and maintained a relationship with only *one* person from EpiGuide, Michael Ross, who wrote a web serial titled *Footprints*. A few years older than me, Michael became a de facto writing mentor for me and then later a friend (our near-daily texts are mostly about the ludicrous plots on *Days of Our*

Lives, which we've both watched since we were teenagers) as he went on to graduate school and then started a career as a TV writer that I wanted to emulate. He also had a much stronger work ethic than me and published *Footprints* all the fucking time (he still writes it to this day, actually, whereas I bailed on *Guasti Cose* at some point in 2013). Michael's show was quite popular, one of the more popular on EpiGuide, because it was well written but also grounded in real human emotions (it was more of an ABC soap than my *Passions* rip-off). And so, while my series was splashy and quite a few people read it, when it didn't get the "acclaim" from strangers on the internet that I craved, I found another outlet for people discussing my writing that would involve immediate feedback from people whose opinions I craved—AOL Instant Messenger.

As I explained before, AOL Instant Messenger (otherwise known as AIM) was a popular instant messaging platform in the late nineties and early aughts. You could send instant messages to people on your buddy list, and when you were away from your computer, you put up away messages that usually said something like "eating dinner brb" or had pointed song lyrics directed at a crush or a friend, which is what Instagram Stories are mostly used for nowadays.

I partook in the usual usage of AIM for quite a bit until I discovered I could use it as a platform for the writing attention I desperately wanted, so I launched a daily serial titled *Bay City*. I wrote a serial in my away messages every weekday after school, and in the spirit of Carrie Bradshaw and her real-life counterparts Bushnell and Ellis, the fictional serial was loosely based on my friends and classmates at Marquette and its sister school, Divine Savior Holy Angels, only in the series we all attended Bay City High School in Bay City, Wisconsin.

For the most part, the storylines were typical soap opera

clichés. I used to post recaps of the serial on my blog at the time. A recap of the series's debut month, September 2003, reads (unedited) as follows:

At Bay Mall's Barnes & Noble, we are introduced to Michael Sanders as he takes Chris Locke to task for talking with his never-girlfriend, Billie Buckley. Chris tries convincing Billie to go to Homecoming with him, but she won't agree because she correctly thinks Chris's friends hate her. Michael gets Chris to hang up the phone and return to work, then he calls Billie and leaves her a cryptic message. At Suncoast Video, Fallon Fuller shows up to work with a hangover, irritating his co-workers Adam Masters and Bill Archer. When Fallon screws up at work, Bill covers for him with their boss, but gets his own paycheck docked in dealing with the mistake. At Applebee's, Aaron Harder and his girlfriend, Karen Davis, are being served by Cooper O'Connor. Cooper overhears complaining about Shane Douglas becoming captain of the football team. Cooper, who doesn't care about Homecoming but wants to go for fun, suggests to his friend and co-worker, Nick Louis, that they go together. Nick, being closeted, pretends to be homophobic and tells Cooper that he'd feel uncomfortable taking another guy to Homecoming. At the mall's food court, Jake Newman tells Will Patterson about his new punk band. Will is worried about Jake's commitment to their emo band, but Jake insists he can handle two bands. Back at Barnes & Noble, Brian Barnes and Myles Hill discuss voting Fallon onto Homecoming Court. Michael interjects to inform them that he's nominated for Court as well, so they should vote for him. Brian and Myles evade giving Michael an answer, but Michael has already moved on to inform Lance Jay, who's on the Homecoming committee, that he needs to make sure Michael wins Homecoming King, or else there'll be consequences.

It would've been fine enough to write a bad version of *One Tree Hill* or something that was loosely based on my classmates, but then during the summer and fall of 2003, *Days of Our Lives* launched a storyline titled the Salem Stalker, about a serial killer who offed half of the town (they all ended up being secretly alive on an island that was an exact replica of their hometown, Salem, only the island was called Melaswen, which is "New Salem" backward), and then I got the idea to *also* do a serial killer storyline in *Bay City*.

Which prompted me to introduce someone named the Bay City Shooter, who was offing my classmates. I'm shocked the FBI didn't arrest me.* To be a high school student in the early 2000s meant that you lived through the Columbine shooting, where two high school students, Dylan Klebold and Eric Harris, murdered twelve students and one teacher on the morning of April 20, 1999, at Columbine High School in Littleton, Colorado. After the incident, they both committed suicide in the school library. It was, at the time, a huge, horrific deal, and the deadliest mass shooting at a high school in United States history, until the Parkland High School shooting in 2018. But back in 1999, the idea that two people would shoot up a school was shocking. It might be hard to understand that if you're a high school student now, where the concept of dodging bullets during active shooter drills is about as commonplace as a new Taylor Swift album.

* They did visit school, though, when one of my classmates was planning to blow up our social studies teacher with a pipe bomb. It did not become a bigger deal because most people understood the impetus.

Immediately after Columbine, when I was still in middle school, we would frequently wait outside for thirty minutes to an hour in the morning because someone had called in a bomb threat. Because of the rumor that Klebold and Harris were goths and loners with no friends, every kid at school who also fit that description had a target on them. They were supposedly godless worshippers of Satan, if you believed the (later-revealed-to-be-untrue) story that Harris murdered one of his victims because she responded yes to the question "Do you believe in God?" In actuality, they had friends at school, and they weren't loners. They also happened to be psychopaths who dreamed of becoming famous by killing a bunch of their classmates. But as we headed into the early 2000s, it was commonplace to think that wearing all black clothing and listening to Marilyn Manson meant that you wanted to shoot up your school.

Not that people didn't play into the stereotype—I can remember a handful of kids who were pulled into the principal's office because they had "hit lists," or lists of classmates who they hated and wanted to kill. Which is why it's surprising to me that my very public teen soap opera based on my classmates that then depicted a storyline that involved the murder of those classmates by a mysterious serial killer did *not* get me pulled into the principal's office.

But then again, I never appeared on a single hit list post-Columbine either. At the time, I wondered if that meant I wasn't important enough. You mean none of my classmates hate me enough to want to kill me? Am I not popular? That's the type of thing that will lead you to start writing thinly veiled accounts of your friends' lives, because if they don't find you important, then you'll make yourself important.

Actors don't like to play coma. They feel it limits their range.

—ROSE SCHWARTZ, *SOAPDISH* (1991)

· · · · ·

WHOOPI

My conversion to Judaism was even quicker than Kristin Davis's Charlotte York's on *Sex and the City* when she married divorce attorney Harry Goldenblatt. No, I'm not actually Jewish, but I have been asked if I am on more than one occasion due to having the name Ira.

The first time was at a seder with Mom's co-worker Janet, where her son was confused about why I had a Jewish name. I shrugged and said maybe I'm Jewish, because why not "yes, and . . ." your ethnicity if the boy asking you about it is cute. Unfortunately, one thing Mom and I have in common is we cycled through best friends in our thirties, so after a few family gatherings, I never saw Janet or her hot Jewish son again. I mourn the relationship that could have been, if only because I could've written a teenage gay Black version of *The Last Five Years* and been an Obie Award winner already.

In actuality, the name Ira comes from my uncle Ira, a staff sergeant in the Marines who died in a car accident five months before I was born. And if I don't feel that bad about pretending to be Jewish, it's partially because my entire name feels like a fabrication—I'm the third Ira Lee in my family, but certainly not by any paternal lineage like the royalty I read about in Shakespeare plays. But "Ira Madison III" is on my birth certificate, so c'est la vie.

My lie about my name reminds me of Whoopi Goldberg's adoption of a Jewish surname. Whoopi (as I've mentioned before, one of my gran's faves) has long said her surname belongs to a Jewish ancestor and that she feels just as Jewish as she does Black,* but also, in a 2006 episode of the PBS series *African American Lives* where Henry Louis Gates Jr. traces the lineage of Goldberg and several other celebrities like Chris Tucker and Quincy Jones . . . no Jewish lineage was discovered.

But I'm sure a ballsy move like arriving in Hollywood and forging your own mythology (it worked for every white Golden Age of Hollywood actor, including Roy Harold Scherer Jr., who you probably know as Rock Hudson) is what made Goldberg so admirable to Gran. When I look at Whoopi, I see my gran. They're both women who dress casually—comfortably—like they've just spent the afternoon working in the garden. I'm ashamed of the times I ever found myself embarrassed by Gran's modern-day Brooklyn-lesbian attire, especially given what I wear daily now. I thought of her on the day I watched *The View* and Goldberg referred to a reporter who criticized her wardrobe as "an anonymous bitch."

Both my gran and Goldberg have had troubled histories with white partners in the nineties—Thomas, my gran's on-again, off-again boyfriend, never dressed up in blackface at a Friars Club roast like Ted Danson did, but he and I did trade barbs often enough that I now look back and realize I was auditioning for a Problem Child film while also being overly territorial

* Though someone who "feels Jewish" might not have claimed that the Holocaust wasn't originally about race, like she did in 2022, when she referred to the Holocaust as "white-on-white violence." After a suspension from *The View*, Goldberg apologized in a statement: " 'The Holocaust was about the Nazis' systematic annihilation of the Jewish people—who they deemed to be an inferior race.' I stand corrected."

of Gran, because I had already moved out of my mom's house and didn't want to lose the stability in the new home I'd finally found. After Gran and Thomas's relationship ended, though, Thomas stayed in our lives and even gave my gran money when she needed it for my school and college expenses, which is more than I deserved. When asked about marriage, Gran mostly lived a life akin to Goldberg's viral 2016 quote in a *New York Times* interview: "I don't want somebody in my house."

Before Goldberg was cussing out white women daily on *The View*, she played every role an actor could imagine—she was an action star, a comedian, a cop in a thriller, the lead in a Spielberg period drama, a psychic, a lead in a musical, a white man, and an alien, and she starred opposite a CGI dinosaur (maybe no one really wanted that, but I'm sure the check was good). Among the various VHS tapes that littered my gran's house, the woman on the cover of most of them was Goldberg.

The Color Purple (1985). The Spielberg adaptation of Alice Walker's novel, which was essentially America's introduction to Goldberg. Before that, she'd had a one-woman show on Broadway and had done theater in California, but this was her big-budget feature-film debut. Showing how circular time is and how very little changes, in a *Chicago Sun-Times* interview with Roger Ebert, Oprah insisted that Goldberg would get an Oscar for the film: "Who's her competition? Meryl Streep? I don't care if Meryl break-dances on water; this year it's Whoopi."

Streep has been terrorizing actresses for years, apparently, and she *was* nominated against Goldberg for Best Actress for *Out of Africa*, which is a romantic drama about white people in Africa. If that sounds snide, it's not; it's just a literal description of a movie that is good but is also from Streep's most boring era of film, her late-eighties and early-nineties dramas. Meanwhile, any Streep comedy from that era—*Postcards from the*

Edge, Defending Your Life, Death Becomes Her, and *She-Devil**—
could feasibly be featured at the top of a Best Streep Performances list. Both Streep and Goldberg lost to Geraldine Page in
The Trip to Bountiful, which is a film I will never watch because
Cicely Tyson brought me to tears in the 2013 Broadway production and I don't need to see the white version.

In 2010 Goldberg and Oprah had a sit-down on Oprah's
show to address their rumored beef, since they hadn't remained
friends since *The Color Purple* and Goldberg was noticeably absent from Oprah's Legends Ball in 2006, where she invited
damn near every famous Black woman over the age of fifty. I
love Black women, because even though Oprah made Diana
Ross and Patti LaBelle and Gladys Knight squash *their* beef on
TV, she wasn't about to air *her* business like that. The sit-down
with Whoopi amounted to them both saying, "Well, I thought
you hated me!" and that they had never said a disparaging word
against each other. This wasn't about to be an Andy Cohen
Bravo reunion. They cried and squashed the beef none of us
had even known about, but it was yet another life lesson from
Oprah about sharing just a little bit of your life publicly, but not
too much.

Jumpin' Jack Flash (1986). I remember two things about this
film—the poster where Goldberg is literally flying in the air
doing a jumping jack (but the movie isn't about jumping jacks;
it's about a British spy named Jumpin' Jack Flash who needs
Goldberg's help escaping a Russian prison) and the fact that she
dresses up as Tina Turner to escape spies in the film. The movie
is a prolonged Rolling Stones joke, essentially making it the
"Moves Like Jagger" of the eighties.

---

* *She-Devil* is a horrible film, with the worst performance belonging to Roseanne Barr, but Streep is amazing in it.

But unlike a crazy viral 2021 meme that jokes that before joining *The Voice* and making that song with co-host Adam Levine, Christina Aguilera was "at her lowest . . . fat, nasty and broke. Career in shambles. She came on this bitch mad as hell!!!,"* this movie was the opposite for Goldberg following her Oscar-nominated turn in *The Color Purple*. It did her no favors and led to *Fatal Beauty* (1987), an awful rip-off of *Beverly Hills Cop* and a PSA about testing your cocaine for fentanyl where Goldberg plays a wisecracking narcotics detective who has a romance with Sam Elliott, which only exists now as a time capsule of how hot Elliott was. Also, Goldberg punches a yuppie white woman in the gut, which had to have been cathartic for Black audiences in 1987.

Ghost (1990). I was baptized in a Baptist church and went to a Jesuit high school and college, but the thing that has seeped into my mind as a religious text more than any of those was this film where Goldberg played a fake psychic who was visited by a real ghost, a dead Patrick Swayze attempting to warn his girlfriend, Demi Moore, that he had been murdered by criminals who were coming after her. In this film, good people go into the light and presumably to heaven unless they have unfinished business, like Swayze—then you have to take pottery classes with your girlfriend until she realizes your ghost is trying to tell her something.

But the bad people? Their souls are *immediately* dragged all

---

* As with most joke tweets about pop singers, you have to take it all with a grain of salt. In actuality, Maroon 5's 2010 *Hands All Over* flopped prior to a reissue that included "Moves Like Jagger." Aguilera, as the highest-paid judge on *The Voice*, actually helped the album go platinum. This is not to say that Aguilera's 2010 album, *Bionic*, fared any better on the charts, but *Bionic* is an iconic flop that gay millennials still listen to. *Hands All Over* is just a god-awful album, and this is coming from a publicly admitted Maroon 5 fan.

the way to hell. I was half paying attention to this film the first time I watched it as a kid, but the moment that the bad guys are dragged to hell at the conclusion of the film scarred me more than any theology class that told me being a faggot was evil. Goldberg won a Supporting Actress Oscar for this film (Meryl was nominated that year too, but for Best Actress, and she lost to Kathy Bates in *Misery*, which is kind of iconic, given what the Oscars award these days).

Soapdish (1991). A comedy set behind the scenes of a daytime soap opera. I don't know if there was a single film that spoke to me more as a kid than this. It stars Sally Field (one of Black people's ten fave white celebs) as a soap star who's trying to be ousted from the show by Robert Downey Jr. (*Iron Man* saved his career, but it's a shame Gen Z only knows him as a man who flies around in a suit). In a movie that's endlessly quotable, my favorite quote might be Whoopi (who plays the soap's head writer) talking about why she can't bring a character back to *The Sun Also Sets*: "He was driving in the Yukon, in a pink convertible, to visit his brother who's an ex-con named Frances, when a tractor trailer comes along and decapitates him. You know what that means? It means he doesn't have a head. How am I supposed to write for a guy who doesn't have a head?"

Unfortunately for the film's legacy, it ends on a rather transphobic note, when Field's rival at the network, Cathy Moriarty, is revealed to be trans on air, and Downey Jr. is visibly disgusted because he's been having sex with her. I don't advocate for most films being remade, but I would love a *Soapdish* redo. Unfortunately, the relevance of soap operas today versus 1991 is vastly different.

Sister Act (1992) / *Sister Act 2: Back in the Habit* (1993). This is where I confess something that feels shameful. I have seen the original *Sister Act* more than I've seen the sequel, and that is why whenever people want to do a sing-along to "Joyful, Joyful" from the finale, I usually just nod and mouth along to the words. For some reason, Whoopi on the run from the Mob appeals to me more than Whoopi teaching inner-city kids how to sing praise music. Both are fantastic films, but on-the-run-from-the-Mob films might be one of my favorite genres (see also *Some Like It Hot* and *Connie and Carla*).

Sarafina! (1992). I actually never watched this one because it looked like a movie where I was supposed to "learn" something, like with most films from the nineties that were set in Africa, but I do remember the exclamation point and being confused when I saw a bunch of restaurants named Serafina in New York and briefly thought Goldberg had a career as a restauranteur.

Corrina, Corrina (1994). This is like a Disney version of *All That Heaven Allows* where Ray Liotta falls for his Black nanny, Goldberg, in 1959. There's racial tension, obviously, but it all works out in the end. As a melodrama, this film could be a classic, but as a nineties feel-good movie about race, it's just fine.

Boys on the Side (1995). A road trip movie starring Goldberg, Drew Barrymore, and Mary-Louise Parker sounds like a fever dream now. The fact that Goldberg also plays a lesbian, Parker's character has AIDS, and Barrymore is struggling with an abusive relationship makes it seem like a contrived tearjerker, but it's a rare film that has three female leads with completely distinctive, original personalities that are imbued with life and heart by fantastic actresses. They, quite literally, do not make films like *Boys on the Side* anymore.

The film was written by my former co-worker Don Roos, who I worked with on the Netflix series *Uncoupled*. He also wrote the very iconic *Single White Female* (you might be more familiar with the equally iconic rip-off, 2011's *The Roommate*), where Bridget Fonda's new roommate, Jennifer Jason Leigh, becomes not only obsessed with her but obsessed with *becoming* her. The entire film is worth it for the shot when Leigh walks in wearing the same haircut as Fonda.

Eddie (1996) and *The Associate* (1996), released eight months apart, are two films I often confuse for each other. These wildly different movies are nineties feminist fantasies (meaning they were written and directed by men), and both deal with Goldberg taking on traditional male roles as a woman. In *Eddie*, Goldberg plays a Knicks fan who ends up becoming the team's coach. In *The Associate*, Goldberg invents a white man named Cutty to be her business partner to combat sexism at work. At a certain point, Goldberg must enlist her queer friends to put her in drag as a white man.

The Associate is my second-favorite ridiculous storyline about a woman dressing up in prosthetics as a man, the first being a 2005 plot on *Days of Our Lives* where Alison Sweeney's character, Sami, dresses up as a man named Stan in order to get revenge on her enemies. This was done because Sweeney was on maternity leave, and the character of Stan was played by actor Dan Wells, who had previously been on the short-lived Bravo dating series *Boy Meets Boy* in 2003, where a gay man tries to find a partner among fifteen suitors, but the twist is that half the men are straight, and if he picks a straight man, *he* gets the prize money. The lead, James Getzlaff, did ultimately pick a gay man. Shockingly, they are not still together! Love is dead.

How Stella Got Her Groove Back (1998). A precursor to *Girls Trip* in that it's a movie about Black women going on a vacation for sex and love that was popular with audiences but still hasn't spurred any other studios to make similar films, *Stella* stars Angela Bassett as a woman with no sex life whose friend, Goldberg, encourages her to go to Jamaica and find a man. The romance with Taye Diggs, a younger man, is ho-hum compared to the chemistry between Goldberg and Bassett as leads. It's criminal the two haven't reunited on-screen since, possibly in a film where Bassett, an actress, convinces her single friend Goldberg to leave the daytime talk show she's been on for what seems like a century and go on a vacation.

Girl, Interrupted (1999). Goldberg is fantastic in this film as the head nurse at a psychiatric hospital where Winona Ryder ends up after an alleged suicide attempt. Ryder befriends a diagnosed sociopath patient played by Angelina Jolie in my introduction to Jolie on film. Jolie won Best Supporting Actress for this role, and it made her A-list, though she'd already been racking up attention in films like *Hackers* and *The Bone Collector*. In the latter, she stars opposite Denzel Washington in a thriller that follows a tried-and-true formula for thrillers from the late nineties and early aughts—pairing a white ingenue with an older Black man. Usually, it's Morgan Freeman (paired with Ashley Judd in *Kiss the Girls* and *High Crimes* and with Monica Potter in *Along Came a Spider*).

One thing that seems to have been forgotten in this current famine of A-list stars is that there's white famous, and then there's Black famous. Actors who might be immediately familiar to white audiences might not be familiar to Black audiences and vice versa. But someone *truly* catapults to A-list (à la Jolie) when they can draw audiences of all races to theaters, and nothing did that quicker than pairing a white actor with a popular Black one. From the moment Jolie starred in *The Bone Collector*, she became my gran's favorite actress.

But there was a brief period when Black actors could command a box office independently, without needing to star opposite a white person to draw sales. In the eighties, Eddie Murphy accomplished this with the Beverly Hills Cop franchise, and in the nineties, Whoopi Goldberg did the same. Ironically, her film that tried to replicate Murphy's success, *Fatal Beauty*, was a flop. Usually, playing a cop was an easy way for white audiences to find a Black actor "safe." They were playing authority figures; they were still reinforcing the law and order and checks and balances that white people needed Black people to be boxed into. But somehow Goldberg became so much more than that—a lounge singer, a nun, a lesbian, a medium, a basketball coach, an Oscar nominee—just by being herself.

I'm going to do you the way you did me, and when I'm done,
all you'll be left with is that proverbial wish . . . that you'd
never been born.

—AMANDA WOODWARD, *MELROSE PLACE* (1994)

· · · · ·

MONDAYS ARE A BITCH

The last time I visited Milwaukee, Gran and I watched the
2010 cinematic masterpiece *Salt*. Ever since I was a teenager, she always referred to Angelina Jolie as "her girl," and
nothing has changed since then.

Salt, one of Jolie's last action-hero roles since her humani-
tarian efforts took precedence over acting (I am pretending
Marvel's *Eternals* does not exist), is not just one of my favorite
films but also one that represents so much of Hollywood's
wasted potential. It was originally written for Tom Cruise but
rewritten for Jolie after he dropped out. In it, she plays CIA
operative Evelyn Salt, who is revealed to be a Russian sleeper
agent. A moderate success, *Salt* has grown to cult status online
(fueled mostly by me) but still hasn't produced a sequel fourteen years later. Never mind that if a man were the lead, we'd
probably have six *Salt* sequels by now.

This is Jolie's *Mission: Impossible*. Her *Indiana Jones*. And yet,
despite her skill as an action heroine (honed in the two Tomb
Raider films she made in the early 2000s), an Oscar for 1999's
Girl, Interrupted, and a nomination for 2008's *Changeling* (one of
Clint Eastwood's few directorial bangers, the others being *Un-*

forgiven and *Mystic River*), Jolie has rarely received the roles and accolades from the industry that she deserves.

But she always got accolades from Gran—especially in Jolie's era of being a Hollywood "bad girl": Her brief marriage to Jonny Lee Miller. Her messy relationship with Billy Bob Thornton, which involved intense horniness on red carpets* and wearing vials of each other's blood around their necks. Her alleged affair with and subsequent marriage to Brad Pitt. Her split with Pitt, which garnered much of the same "blame Jolie" press that she earned when she was accused of stealing him from Jennifer Aniston. In regard to that scandal, by the way, we were firmly Team Jolie in Gran's house. To quote Nicki Minaj's (now-outdated) rap from "Stupid Hoe" on 2012's *Pink Friday: Roman Reloaded*, "I'm Angelina, you Jennifer. C'mon, bitch, you see where Brad at?"

Jolie is a white woman, but her dark hair and full lips made her seem "exotic." In the early 2000s, the media referred to anyone who was not a petite blonde as an "exotic beauty." It's why it's now shocking to look at old photos of Jennifer Lopez, who had a perfectly normal curvy figure that was blown out of proportion as the biggest ass to ever grace Hollywood. Angelina was very open with her sexuality, blunt when it came to discussing her disinterest in a traditional marriage, and honest about her struggles with depression and mental health, which pop up in unexamined sound bites in interviews like her 2001 *Rolling Stone* profile: "[Angelina] found [a journal] the other day from when she was fourteen . . . There is the word HELL and a picture of the devil, and there is a ripped-out page [where] the only word remaining is SUICIDE."

---

* The blueprint for Megan Fox and Machine Gun Kelly's red carpet make-outs.

During the afternoons I spent at Barnes & Noble flipping through magazines in between lunch at the food court and a movie matinee, I would devour cover stories that featured my favorite actors. I remember reading that particular issue before seeing the first Tomb Raider film (and sneaking into the R-rated *Swordfish* after, which was being heavily promoted with a scene that promised to show Halle Berry's breasts, but I was mostly interested because Berry was Storm from the previous summer's *X-Men*). Jolie seemed relatable to me—like she intuitively understood the character that introduced me to her in *Girl, Interrupted*.

Girl, Interrupted stars Winona Ryder as a psychiatric-hospital patient who is committed against her will due to nearly dying from a combo of pills and alcohol. I never made an actual suicide attempt as a teenager that would stick beyond one particularly depressing high school night spent wondering if I could overdose on ibuprofen and Svedka vodka—I did not; I fell asleep and woke up in the middle of the night vomiting it all up—but reading Jolie's memories of her journal reminded me of some of the darker things that flashed in my mind and my writing when I wanted an escape from life. When I hated my body. When I hated my face. When I hated my growing attraction to boys and being forced to attend a school that felt like it would eventually expose that. I couldn't make myself disappear, so I made myself disappear in women like Angelina Jolie, the women my gran and I bonded over.

I remember my first picture day at Marquette University High School. The school required you to dress in a collared shirt with a tie. It was a hot August. At least with a loose T-shirt, I could find a way to hide my body from the new influx of skinny, athletic white boys I was suddenly surrounded by. All throughout middle school, I interacted with a variety of races and bodies, but at Marquette, there were the muscular white football players, toned white basketball players, and even more toned white swimmers. I looked nothing like them, and even the handful of other Black kids at Marquette were on sports teams too.

I was the only fat Black kid with thick Harry Potter glasses, comic books in his bag, and *Buffy* recording on the VCR at home. I remember orientation day, when I was still upset about attending this school instead of any of the public schools in the city with people I knew from middle school. I had a permanent scowl on my face when my gran, fed up with my attitude, asked me, "Why can't you be like these white boys who are being nice to their parents?" "Be like the white boys" was a mantra that stuck in my head as I sweated through my entire dress shirt before I sat for my class photo. The scowl from orientation day returned, and with a *click, flash* of the camera, it immortalized me with a scowl and sweat stain in my school photos and eventual yearbook photo. I never had any inclination to emulate the white boys at school.

But the white women my gran and I watched on TV? Yes. Angelina Jolie was far from the only white woman constantly on the TV screen in our house.

Buffy the Vampire Slayer debuted on the now-defunct network the WB* in the spring of 1997 and quickly became (and still is) my favorite TV series. Joss Whedon based the series on his 1992 cult classic movie of the same name, which starred Kristy

---

* The WB was a network mostly full of white teen soap operas and comedies. Another network at the time, UPN, was mostly full of Black comedies. In 2001, *Buffy* switched networks to UPN (along with the alien-focused teen soap *Roswell*) as that network tried to lure in younger white audiences. In 2006, both networks merged to form the CW.

Swanson, *Beverly Hills, 90210*'s Luke Perry, and *Pee-wee's Play-house*'s Paul Reubens. The latter two died recently, whereas Swanson's career is just dead after a heel turn into becoming an alt-right nutjob. The premise of *Buffy* is the same as the film: A ditzy blond cheerleader finds out that she is an every-generation warrior destined to save the world from vampires and demons. The show would eventually add zombies, gods, and Evil itself to Buffy's rogues' gallery, but in its inception, it was about Buffy Summers moving to Sunnydale after being kicked out of her previous school (her backstory was loosely based on the events of the film) and forming a relationship with high school out-casts Willow and Xander and her school librarian Giles, who was her Watcher, a man trained to teach vampire slayers how to, well, slay vampires.

I missed the series' first season, which debuted as a mid-season replacement in March, but I became hooked during summer's repeat airings. This ragtag team of heroes became my best friends, the people I most looked forward to spending the week with.

In the fall of 1997, *Buffy* aired on Monday nights before it moved to Tuesdays in 1998. Unfortunately for me, this was be-fore I had a TV in my room, and therefore control of the TV was a battlefield. Before you could just catch your favorite TV show on streaming the next morning or save it to DVR,* you

---

* In 1999, a digital video recorder called TiVo debuted with a cartoon TV as its mascot. To use it, you attached a device essentially the same size as a VCR to your TV set, and it could record TV series for you. And when you used it, it made a loud cartoon *blip!* noise. I had a TiVo of my own, which I used to record TV once I started doing theater after school. Eventually it broke and I missed the entire second season of *Friday Night Lights*. The second season was derided for a melodramatic storyline where two characters kill an attempted rapist and hide his body. It was maligned at the time, but rewatching it years later, I kinda found it funny.

had to either watch it live or record it on a VCR. To record a TV series, you'd purchase blank VHS tapes (and make sure you bought the ones that could record eight hours instead of two) and set your VCR to record a show.

The only problem was that it could not record multiple channels at once. This was a plus for TV networks in an era where many shows became "hits" simply because people were too lazy to change the channel after their favorite show was on (*Friends* became successful in its first season this way by airing between *Mad About You* and *Seinfeld* before it was popular enough to move to eight p.m. and anchor NBC's Thursday nights). At my most nightmarish and TV-obsessed, I would call my gran from school during theater rehearsal and tell her she needed to change the channel on the TV in my room so that I could record a show on a different network. But on Monday nights in 1997, before I had any interest in theater, I was at home at nine p.m. when *Buffy* aired. The only problem? My favorite white woman was on the air at the same time as another one of my gran's favorite white women: Ally McBeal.

Ally McBeal debuted in the fall of 1997, a week before *Buffy*'s second season began, so I was at home to watch the premiere of David E. Kelley's story about a Boston law firm starring Calista Flockhart alongside a bunch of sex-starved yuppies who took on insane legal cases and (in a modern-day conservative's worst nightmare) shared a unisex bathroom where the men and women of the firm often interacted with or spied on one another's conversations (unisex bathrooms are not only inclusive, they're Shakespearean).

One thing Ally wanted was a *man*. Everyone was obsessed with sex on the show, especially Ally. Referred to as "problematic" and the opposite of a role model by Emily Nussbaum in *The New Yorker*, Ally was infamously on a 1998 *Time* cover (in color, alongside black-and-white photos of Susan B. Anthony, Betty Friedan, and Gloria Steinem) above the headline "Is Feminism Dead?"* Believe it or not, Ally did not kill feminism, but the chief complaints about the series were that it was a male's fantasy of women. Ally wore insanely short skirts to the office, was obsessed with her ex-boyfriend despite him being in a new relationship, and had fantasies about her breasts growing larger.

And yet the show was extremely popular among women, including my gran. I can't speak to why women were drawn to stories written by men, but on *Ally McBeal* you could quite literally see Ally's fantasies played out on-screen. She had a fabulous job, looked gorgeous, and had insecurities that made her relatable, and we got to see literal depictions of those insecurities on the screen every week. It was inspirational but also relatable. She wasn't a "boss" who sacrificed her love life for men; she wanted to have it all, and that appealing wish fulfillment is why people still watch the Real Housewives to this day.

Since *Ally McBeal* aired at the same time as *Buffy* in the fall of 1997, I recorded *Buffy* on VHS, and we would watch it after *Ally*. In a way, the shows were very similar. Both trafficked in female wish fulfillment where young blond women were allowed to fight back against the world that attacked them. And in *Buffy*'s case, being a vampire slayer gave her incredible strength that allowed her to still wear miniskirts and flirt with boys while hiding the fact that she fought vampires and demons every night. Sure, she had to wash blood and dirt out of her hair every night, but to me, Buffy Summers was everything.

There's a reason *Buffy* has so many queer fans beyond the

---

* Whenever *Time* magazine ran out of cover material then, they liked to ask, "Is feminism dead?" to get women fired up to respond. It was the nineties version of writing something incendiary on Twitter for clicks.

fact that it had literal queer representation in characters like Willow, who comes out in the series' fourth season. Buffy had to hide her identity from her parents and people at school, which felt a lot like the journey of me, a queer kid in Milwaukee who had his own secrets to bear. And watching that in conjunction with *Ally McBeal* felt like a sign that the adult world meant I would be able to experience a life with much more freedom than the constraints of high school allowed. After all, it was sort of an unspoken rule for millennial queer kids at the time that you stayed in the closet till college. In college, there seemed to be a wealth of freedom not dissimilar to the unisex bathrooms and your wildest fantasies playing out like Ally's.

Each week, my gran and I sat to watch the exploits of these blond women, a tradition in my family for as long as I can remember—discussing the exploits of blond women, that is. Though "my soap" has always been *Days of Our Lives*, a ritual that has continued to this day even though the show has moved to streaming on Peacock, the first daytime soap I watched with my family was *The Young and the Restless*. Whether I was at my gran's house or my aunt Ruth's house or my great-grandmother's house in Elkhart (my extended family would stop by and gossip during commercial breaks and shout at the screen) or even the barbershop (the amount of straight Black men who seemed to remember *Y&R* stories from the nineties is shocking), when eleven-thirty a.m. hit, Victor Newman was on the TV screen.

If you grew up in a Black household in the nineties, you know who Victor Newman is. A cold-hearted businessman who lived in Genoa City, Wisconsin, he was written into the series in 1980 for a short stint. He quickly became one of the series' most popular characters, thanks in part to his ruthlessness, as seen when he discovered his wife Julia was having an affair with a fashion photographer, so Victor had the man kid-napped and locked him in a bomb shelter in the basement of his ranch. Victor was wicked, but he was also incredibly sexy and charismatic, and when he next set his sights on blond strip-per Nikki Reed, two stars were born. Nikki was portrayed by Melody Thomas Scott, who can only be described as a blond bombshell. Harkening back to a kind of old-Hollywood glam-our, the films that my grandparents grew up with, she quickly became just as ubiquitous in the series as Victor.

Soaps are known for the exaggerated melodrama, glamor-ous wardrobes (not currently, though—the remaining soaps on the air are on an ASOS budget), and intense close-ups. My fa-vorite soap opera camera technique involves a close-up of a character in the foreground and a blurry character standing be-hind them who then comes into focus as the foreground blurs. It's a simple yet incredibly effective shot that gives you two characters' intense emotions in one shot, and no one was bet-ter than Scott at serving you face with perfect tens across the board in a dramatic scene.

Even feminist scholar Camille Paglia, a lover of soaps, praised Scott in the foreword to Scott's memoir, *Always Young and Restless*. "Melody Thomas Scott may be the last great prac-titioner of the soap genre—unless and until a new generation of young actors picks up the torch. Melody accepts and cele-brates the unique protocols of her artistic process: as she frankly admits, soaps 'exaggerate': 'Our medium is often *not* based in reality.' "*

---

* Although I would give this distinction to legend Deidre Hall as well, who has portrayed Marlena Evans on *Days of Our Lives* since 1976, but Paglia admitted on the early-nineties E! talk show *Pure Soap* that she didn't watch *Days*. The show is much campier than *Y&R*, however, so maybe she hated *Days* because she assumed her mortal enemy, Susan Sontag, liked it.

Every afternoon the women in my family (and my great-grandfather) would be glued to the TV, and then they would debate the actions of the characters they'd just watched. They loved the dastardly Jack Abbott, who was often Victor's rival in business and for Nikki's affection, but they always knew Nikki belonged with Victor. And so did the show, which always brought Nikki and Victor back into each other's orbits because of their undeniable chemistry. For me, however, Nikki was too sweet. Even though she had a cruel streak, especially when she drank, she generally had Victor's love, even when they weren't together.

For me, I was drawn to bitches. On Monday nights before *Ally McBeal* aired, *Melrose Place* was on Fox. The show stars Heather Locklear, who plays the blond advertising exec Amanda Woodward. And what was Amanda? A bitch. She ruined the lives of business rivals, romantic rivals, and even the men in her life. People loved her so much that when the show moved to Monday nights, Fox advertised the series with ads of Locklear's face and the tagline "Mondays are a bitch."

But as much as I admired Amanda, she was more in line with a universe that Ally McBeal lived in. She was an adult; she had more freedom than I did. I didn't relate to her the way that I did to Buffy Summers. But Buffy fulfilled the good-angel role on one shoulder, the girl with a secret who fought on the side of the white hats. I soon found myself with an opposing devil on my shoulder the first time I saw *Days of Our Lives*. My grandmother wasn't a regular *Days* watcher, but she must've watched it from time to time, because she knew most of the characters on the show. And the first time I saw the show in the nineties, the person who caught my attention was Sami Brady.

Sami Brady, played by Alison Sweeney, who most millennials will recognize as the host of *The Biggest Loser*, an NBC show where trainers yell at fat people to lose weight in a deranged reality-TV contest (as an actual fat kid, the show scared me, and I never watched it), was the daughter of Deidre Hall's Marlena Evans. She was always in competition with her perfect older sister, Carrie, particularly for the love of town idiot Austin Reed. One night, Sami witnesses her mother having an affair with John Black, and it forever changes the course of her life. She transforms, under the writing of head writer James E. Reilly (who would later create *Passions*), into a scheming, raging, cold-hearted bitch.

She constantly plots to break up Carrie and Austin, even going as far as drugging Austin to make him believe he is having sex with her sister and then claiming the baby she has afterward is Austin's (it is actually Austin's brother Lucas's, which is exposed, after years of lies, at Sami and Austin's wedding). Sami was relatable to every teenager who had dreams deferred, and instead of moping about them like Claire Danes on *My So-Called Life*, she just decides to manipulate the entire town of Salem to get whatever she wants.

I think about the lyrics to "Inner White Girl" from the musical *A Strange Loop* quite a bit, where the lead character Usher bemoans how he wasn't born a white girl. He sings, "White girls can do anything, can't they? Black boys must always obey their mothers." I can appreciate the sentiment that as Black boys, queer or otherwise, you always fall prey to society's expectations in a way that white girls do not in America. There's a freedom to be reckless and make mistakes, with the knowledge that the country bends over backward to protect you. But I never craved the feeling of wanting an inner white girl because I craved some soft life. I was drawn to Buffy because of her hardness; I wanted the ability to kick someone's ass. And I was drawn to Sami because I wanted the ability to get whatever

I wanted by any means necessary. And on TV in the nineties, the only people who had the ability to achieve any of those goals were largely white women.

Even when my gran was young, white women were the model. Even in influential groups like the Supremes, there was always the idea that Diana Ross and her bandmates had to re-create the poise, elegance, and softness of whiteness to gain popularity. It's probably why Gran said it was so important for me to emulate the white boys at school, to be like them, to hide my scowls. "Be like the boys who play Beatles songs on their guitars during lunch." I fucking hated the Beatles. It's a common joke among millennials like myself to drag the Beatles for being overrated, but this isn't that. During one of our school Kairos retreats, I was awoken every morning to "Here Comes the Sun" blaring on the speakers. Even when the crush I had, Kevin, the sweet, curly-haired diabetic straight boy who often sang Beatles songs (his favorites were "Yesterday" and "Hey Jude"), whipped out his guitar, he couldn't make me love them—but I did pretend to love them to hang out with him.

At some point, after listening to them enough times to keep up conversation with white boys, I began to genuinely love the Beatles. In rotation were the dreamy, percussion-heavy pop songs from their earlier catalog that didn't require experience with hallucinogens to be enamored of. Particularly "Michelle," written by Paul McCartney with assistance from John Lennon, who told *Playboy* in 1980 that when it came to his and McCartney's writing partnership, Lennon contributed the "sadness, the discords, a certain bluesy edge" to McCartney's lightness and optimism.

Growing up in a household where the backdrop to my

mom's turbulent romantic life was the warbles of Mary J. Blige and Aaliyah CDs, I was drawn to songs that had a rougher edge, an inspiration rooted in Black musical traditions rather than white after-school lo-fi coffee shops (as coffee shops became popular in the nineties and early aughts, our high school adopted a "coffee shop" night, which really just encouraged more white boys to sing badly while playing guitar. Also, I don't know why we were drinking coffee at night in high school). I didn't come to appreciate any Beatles songs until the time I heard them at home, playing from my gran's record collection. I realized "Yesterday" was a beautiful song when I heard Diana Ross and the Supremes cover it on their 1966 album, *I Hear a Symphony*. And that's when I realized that maybe I kinda liked the Beatles—my initial dislike of them was because they represented a whiteness that surrounded me every day at school, and I was craving, in some part, a reclamation of being Black.

I hadn't yet learned how much Black music had inspired most of the white artists my classmates listened to, including Nina Simone inspiring one of the Beatles' best songs, "Michelle." In that same *Playboy* interview, Lennon says the song was initially a joke song intended to be sung partly in French at a party (the "Michelle, ma belle" opening). But after hearing Nina Simone's cover of "I Put a Spell on You," where she put her own emphasis on the "you" in "I love you, I love you," Lennon was prompted to add the same emphasis in the middle of the "I love *you* / I love *you* / I love *YOU*" on the bridge in "Michelle."

Thanks to Simone's influence, "Michelle" finally had something that Paul McCartney's otherwise-beautiful lyrics didn't possess when he first penned the song with Lennon: soul. And then I learned to realize that while the Supremes might have been told to emulate white poise in their performances, it was white artists who'd soon be cribbing from their music.

The Supremes began as the Primettes, a group composed of Diana Ross (who was going to be Diane until a clerical error on her birth certificate led to the name Diana), Florence Ballard, Mary Wilson, and Betty McGlown. Barbara Martin replaced McGlown in 1960 and by 1962 Martin herself exited, leaving us with the trio that has been permanently etched in history. The Supremes sang love songs that were written for them, and they also covered love songs written for other people, like those of the Beatles.

Korean American artist Nam June Paik used his work to show how machines could use images from the past—recent or far—to propel us into the future. I like to think of the Supremes as Afrofuturist. What else correlates to Paik's quote "A culture that's gonna survive is the culture that you can carry around in your head" more than the black-and-white recordings of the Supremes performing on televised pop-music showcases or late-night talk shows in austerely choreographed movements that relied on hand gestures and gentle swaying? Or the records where they sang meticulously crafted love songs from songwriting trio Holland–Dozier–Holland (Swedish pop-music manufacturers like Max Martin have got nothing on them, as much as I love ". . . Baby One More Time" and its successors).

Berry Gordy's vision of the Supremes, and Motown writ large, was of a future where white people listened to the music of Black people. Ross and the Supremes were enrolled in Maxine Powell Finishing and Modeling School to smooth their "snooty" and unsophisticated rough edges. "I told them they had to be trained to appear in the No. 1 places around the country and even before the Queen of England and the president of the United States," Powell told *Vanity Fair* in 2008. Or, as Wesley Morris put it in the 1619 Project's article "Why Is Everyone Always Stealing Black Music?": "Respectability wasn't a problem with Motown; respectability was its point."

The Supremes produced an image of Blackness that was not yet in the public consciousness—an image of Black women in floor-length gowns and evening gloves and perfectly coiffed updos and highly styled shortened bobs. When they sing the love songs of the Beatles, the Supremes take those impersonations of blues and infuse them with a shared heartbreak particular only to Black women in America and to queer Black men like myself who grew up in an environment where emotions and vulnerability were rarely witnessed, and even then, only from the women in my family. Tenderness among men was absent.

My father wasn't in the picture and my great-grandfather was never capable of telling anyone he loved them. His response when my grandmother would tell him "I love you" was "Be sweet." Is it any wonder that once I embraced my queerness and the emancipation that comes with finding your own community, "I love you" became a phrase that easily flew off my tongue? I've never experienced what I might call being *in* love, but my closest friends certainly have heard an emphatic "I love *you* / I love *you* / I love *YOU*" from me.

As a person who does not find it easy to express my emotions unless it's after three a.m. and I'm high at a party or rave in Brooklyn, I tend to use music to hack my own grief and produce tears. Usually to mixed success. Melancholic songs don't make me cry when they should, and even the most saccharine of pop songs have despair nestled in their DNA. Too much of that will just rebound against my emotional wall. So, what am I to do when I just want to let the floodgates open?

When I want to sink into my bed and let myself become over-whelmed with emotion? I return to the music of the Supremes.

For the album art for 1966's *I Hear a Symphony*, Ross, Bal-lard, and Wilson are dimly lit in soft cyan tones, adorned in immaculate bobs, wearing brightly colored lipstick that lands on the frostier side of a nude lip. Ballard is holding a white dove. They're frozen in time and still manage to evoke the image of Blackness unencumbered by the national grief that constantly besieges it. Black people, unfortunately, understand the science fiction trope of a stranger in a strange land far too well, and you can hear it on "Stranger in Paradise," which quite literally begins with the lyrics "Take my hand / I'm a stranger in Paradise." It's a cover of a song from the 1953 musical *Kis-met*, but here it is imbued with much more longing and sorrow.

A haunting melody swells on the night of January 16, 1968, at the Royal Concertgebouw in Amsterdam, Netherlands. Through grainy YouTube footage, I see the Supremes onstage in spar-kly evening gowns adorned with jewels and sleeves. "This is a beautiful number written by some of our favorite composers," Ross says, highlighting the word "composers" as reverence to Lennon and McCartney as they glide into their own renditions of "Michelle" and "Yesterday." McCartney's initial composition of "Michelle" included a jokey imitation of a Frenchman sing-ing. But here, Ross performs the song earnestly, hands clenched into fists, telling the story of a man she *loves*.

When she transitions to "Yesterday," the lyrics are still beau-tiful, but that lightness and optimism are gone. All that's left is the sadness, the discord, that certain bluesy edge Lennon in-fused into the original. Ross's rendition breaks my heart. When she sings, "I said something wrong," she's fighting back tears, constraining her jaw to maintain composure. When I was told be like the white boys at school, what I couldn't tell Gran then, but would soon come to discover after four years at Marquette, was that white boys were hurtful with their words and careless with the emotions of others.

So, when I couldn't disappear into the worlds of my favorite TV shows, to "be like the white boys," I had to learn my own austere choreography to draw attention to myself—just like the Supremes.

Got buffoons eating my pussy while I watch cartoons.

—LIL' KIM, "QUEEN BITCH," *HARD CORE* (1996)

· · · · ·

I USED TO BE SCARED OF THE DICK

I hated nothing more than riding in the car to school with my mom. Even in the dead of winter (Milwaukee winters were Sister Souljah cold), she'd drive with the window rolled down and a cigarette in her hand. She'd usually be blaring a hip-hop album. Biggie, 2Pac, and Jay-Z were in heavy rotation—albums I listen to regularly now, but when I hit my adolescent years, I wasn't interested in anything my mom listened to, as a rule.

This meant that while my classmates were listening to rap music they'd heard on Milwaukee's hip-hop and R&B station V100 or seen on BET and ignoring the oldies their parents listened to, my mom was in her early thirties, so she wasn't listening to "that old stuff" that Gran listened to. Also, rap was aggressively heterosexual. It was all about running through bitches like the Tomb Raider. Never mind the few "faggot"s thrown into the lyrics for seasoning.

That caused me to deep-dive into pop music in middle school, which coincided with the debut of MTV's *Total Request Live*. TRL was a countdown show where viewers voted on their favorite music videos and the top ten most popular ones of the day would air. The series had a set of revolving hosts, with Carson Daly being the most remembered, alongside Dave Holmes, Ananda Lewis, Damien Fahey, Sway, and Jesse Camp, who won

the only season anyone remembers of the MTV reality series
Wanna Be a VJ.

The videos on the countdown ranged from pop to rap to
rock, but when the series debuted it was entrenched in the
most intense cultural debate of 1998. For adults, it was whether
a blow job constituted "sexual relations" as President Bill Clinton was impeached on December 19, 1998, for lying under oath
and obstructing justice after he denied fucking White House
intern Monica Lewinsky. But for anyone under the legal drinking age, the most intense cultural debate of 1998 was Backstreet Boys versus *NSYNC.

Both boy bands were managed by war criminal Lou Pearlman, who in 1993 formed the Backstreet Boys, composed of
AJ McLean, Howie Dorough, Nick Carter, Kevin Richardson,
and Brian Littrell, then stunned the group when he created
a *second* boy band in 1995. That group was *NSYNC, which
consisted of Justin Timberlake, JC Chasez, Joey Fatone, Chris
Kirkpatrick, and Lance Bass. BSB felt betrayed by Pearlman and
parted ways with him, only to be entangled in never-ending
lawsuits against him. (*NSYNC would follow suit, alleging
Pearlman stole money from them as well.) In 2000, both bands
reached the apex of their power—BSB was on the verge of re-
leasing *Black & Blue*, their third U.S. album, just eight months
after *NSYNC released their massive third album, *No Strings Attached*, which sold over 2.4 million U.S. copies in its first week (a
record bested only in 2015 by Adele's *25*). BSB sold only 1.6 million in the United States their first week, but internationally the
album rocked *NSYNC by selling five million in its first week.

The bands' rivalry was fueled by Pearlman in part, but
then by fans and the media as well. For the entirety of *TRL*'s
first six months, from September 1998 to February 1999, BSB
and *NSYNC took turns each week as number one on the

daily video countdown. BSB's "I'll Never Break Your Heart" (a forgettable single, actually) claimed the first two days on the countdown, and *NSYNC's "Tearin' Up My Heart" claimed Wednesday through Friday. For the next six months, those singles battled for the top spot alongside BSB's "All I Have to Give" and *NYSNC's "(God Must Have Spent) A Little More Time on You" and "Merry Christmas, Happy Holidays." They were finally outdone by Korn's "Freak on a Leash" on February 25, 1999, but the battle would resume in just a few weeks when BSB's "I Want It That Way" went head-to-head with *NSYNC's "Thinking of You (I Drive Myself Crazy)" (with a video set in a psych ward that'd be deemed insensitive now). In terms of rivalry, lines in the sand were clearly drawn in U.S. schools. You could listen to both bands, obviously, but you had to pick one band as your fave. Magazine cutouts of that band would be pasted on your notebook or in your locker, with a heavy emphasis on the member you found most attractive.

I was an *NSYNC die-hard, because even though Backstreet Boys had quite a few bops ("The Call," "Shape of My Heart," and "Everybody (Backstreet's Back)" are my go-tos), for the most part they were already auditioning for easy listening radio. Plus, they were far from *boys*. These were grown-ass men, and all the pomp and circumstance of *NSYNC seemed beneath them. Younger girls skewed toward Nick Carter, the youngest of the group. People who have grown up to be gay male adults liked Kevin Richardson, because he gave off daddy vibes. Most girls tended to like Brian Littrell, an infatuation spurred only by him getting open heart surgery in 1998 and being left with a sexy scar on his chest. AJ, the bad boy of the group (he had a lot of tattoos and only talked about having sex with his girlfriend in interviews), had his fans, but those tended to be the BSB fans who skewed older, like college students who could at least get into a bar with a fake ID. One of my friends from middle school, Jessica, was particularly into Howie, but she was weird. But when it came to appreciating their talent, everyone seemed to agree that every member of BSB pulled their own weight.

If you were an *NSYNC fan, more often than debating whether the band was better than BSB, you had to debate which member was the actual star of the group. The obvious choices were Justin Timberlake and JC Chasez. The first album relied heavily on JC's vocals, and there's no denying he's the best singer in the group and the one who, in retrospect, fans wish had been pushed more into the lead role over Timberlake. But Timberlake and his blond curls and the cred you give to the one white boy who hangs out with only Black kids at school (FUBU owner Daymond John had Timberlake as one of the only white celebs publicly wearing the brand to market it to a wider audience) ended up as the star of the group.

To be fair, he did have the charisma and the white-hot celebrity romance when he began dating Britney Spears. This made it more of a Deena-and-Effie-from-*Dreamgirls* situation. JC had the talent, but Justin was *it*. He wouldn't have transitioned into superstardom with a solo career if he weren't. In the mid 2000s, everyone in a boy or girl group who wanted a solo career tried to be either Justin or Beyoncé. Many failed. I suspect it's a bit of revisionist history predicated on Timberlake's involvement in Janet Jackson's Super Bowl incident and her subsequent black-balling from the industry that has made people insist that they were always pushing for JC to be the lead of *NSYNC during its heyday. Yes, JC had that one Blaque song, "Bring It All to Me," where he sang about his Timbz, baggy jeans, and thug appeal, and a dumb song that I nonetheless love called "Blowin' Me Up (With Her Love)" from the *Drumline* soundtrack, but his debut album, *Schizophrenic*, went triple cardboard in 2004 and sold about 52,000 copies in its first week. Y'all weren't really there for my man JC!

The album title was apt because the music is all over the place and none of it sounds geared toward the pop and R&B and hip-hop that were dominating the airwaves at the time in the way that Timberlake's solo debut, *Justified*, was perfectly crafted by Timbaland and the Neptunes. There's maybe *one* good song on *Schizophrenic* ("Come to Me"), and it's a very odd sample of Corey Hart's "Sunglasses at Night." The album was bad, and it cemented that *NSYNC really did only have *one* star. As much as I love JC, he never seemed to *want* to be a pop star as much as Timberlake did, and you can only stan someone into success so far if they don't want it for themselves.

The second most famous member of the band currently is probably Lance Bass, but only because he came out as gay and he loves the spotlight for anything *other* than singing, as he's never attempted a solo career outside of *NYSNC. He did make a decent go of acting, alongside bandmate Joey Fatone, by starring in the 2001 romantic comedy *On the Line*, which he also produced. The film was Bass's plan B after attempts to make *NSYNC's own version of *Spice World* or *A Hard Day's Night* stalled, despite announcing at Cannes in 2000 that they were going to star in a film together, most likely *Grease 3*. They never managed to get the rights to *Grease 3*, and Timberlake was busy plotting his solo career anyway, so Bass and Fatone starred in *On the Line* themselves. As a film, it's horrible, but it's just the right amount of horrible and has such a firm place in early-aughts pop culture that you can probably find someone online claiming it's underrated or one of their favorite films.

Teen pop music became my genre of choice, and it was absolutely nothing my mom or any adult in my life wanted to listen to (except my gran did often borrow my Christina Aguilera CDs, particularly her 1999 self-titled debut and 2000's *My Kind of Christmas*, which is still one of the best Christmas pop albums ever produced—fight someone else about it). Particularly not my grandfather on my dad's side, Henry (also the name of my grandfather on my mom's side), who I stayed with during the summer of 2000 in Vegas before I started high school. Though I'd had no relationship with my dad in about decade, Henry, who we referred to as Papaw, remained in my family's life even when my dad was absent.

When he separated from my dad's mother and relocated to Vegas, I found the perfect way to finally escape Milwaukee—go stay with Papaw for the summer. Traveling for the summer wasn't something that my family did. We rarely attended reunions or even had family vacations. But as I was on the verge of leaving all my friends behind for Marquette and seething with anger at everyone in my family responsible for sending me there, I looked forward to a summer escape hatch.

The thing I remember about Vegas: how unbearably hot it was. As I was already gaining more weight from a lack of social activities, the extra heat of Vegas certainly didn't help either. Stepping outside in the dry desert heat was unbearable, and anytime Papaw drove us anywhere in his dark tangerine Mercury Sable, he had to blast the air-conditioning, but it wasn't enough to keep my skin from sizzling and sticking to his black leather seats (clearly it affected me, however, because I instinctively had to get leather seats when I got my first car, a bright blue Mercedes-Benz).

Papaw worked during the day, but he lived about half a mile from a Tower Records and a movie theater that I frequented every weekend. I saw the highest of art at that movie theater that summer—*X-Men, Coyote Ugly, Scary Movie, The In Crowd* (a horrible teen film that no one of any importance starred in, except for Matthew Settle, who played Rufus Humphrey in *Gossip Girl*, but I knew him as the killer in *I Still Know What You Did Last Summer*), *What Lies Beneath*, and *Nutty Professor II: The Klumps*—on afternoons when I'd stop by Tower Records and then gorge myself on the two-taco combo from Jack in the Box (which sparked my love of that chain restaurant, and it became my go-to DoorDash order in Los Angeles when I was stoned).

But as I said, it was hot as *hell* in summer, and I was still in my hiding-my-body phase of adolescence, so I always had to wear a heavy, baggy shirt that made me sweat even more when I walked to the movies. So I spent most of my time inside watching MTV and *Buffy* reruns and the syndicated airings of S Club 7's two TV shows, *S Club 7 in Miami* and *S Club 7 in LA*. S Club 7 was a British boy/girl band that most popularly spawned the singles "S Club Party" and "Never Had a Dream Come True," but that summer I became obsessed with their single "Natural," which plays in the first episode of the LA series. It would become one of three songs I constantly played on repeat the entire summer and that have been permanently cemented as three of my favorite songs of all the time.

The second was Britney Spears's "Oops! . . . I Did It Again," which debuted on MTV's *Making the Video* on April 10, 2000. There wasn't a bigger person in my life in 2000 than Britney Spears. Her second album, *Oops! . . . I Did It Again*, dropped the same year as *No Strings Attached* and *Millennium*, and the three were the biggest pop acts on MTV at the time (though Aguilera was still making a cultural dent with singles from her debut, it wasn't really until 2002's *Stripped* that she became a phenomenon).

Largely produced by Max Martin, *Oops!* took Spears from a cute girl with a few cute songs to *the moment*. The single was inescapable. She was on the cover of every magazine, transitioning herself from girl next door to sexy pop siren. She had suburban parents all the way mad (the previous year, she posed on the cover of *Rolling Stone* in a bra and panties, clutching a Teletubby) and she had a throng of teenage fans, most of whom would grow up to be gay men, but girls loved her too.

During the summer of 2000, I had yet to attend my first concert but was obsessed with Spears coming to Vegas and begged Papaw to take me. One of his friends, who was taking a daughter of hers, had promised to take me to the Oops! . . . I Did It Again Tour on the August 4 MGM stop. My papaw had told her about me listening to the song nonstop, though I conveniently made sure the times I replayed the video and learned the choreography were only done during the day while he was at work. In one of the biggest disappointments of my life since my dad left us, that friend of his took some random girl who her daughter wasn't even friends with, because "Why would a boy even want to see Britney Spears, anyway?" I've never hated anyone I've never actually met so much in my life.

But remember, "Natural" and "Oops! . . . I Did It Again" were only two of three songs I became obsessed with that summer. On June 20, a video that would quite possibly change the entire course of my life (I wish this were hyperbole, but it's not!) debuted on *TRL*. It was Lil' Kim's "No Matter What They Say." In the music video, Queen Bee sports a series of wigs, the majority of them blond, as she struts in a gold-plated mansion doing choreography with backup dancers, slithering down a brightly lit runway and partying with celeb friends like Diddy, Missy Elliott, Mary J. Blige, and Carmen Electra.

It was the lead single for her second album, *The Notorious*

K.I.M., which took her in a different aesthetic direction than her previous persona, that of a lusty Mob girl, the sexed-up girl-friend of Biggie, who fucked dudes for pleasure and always got the bag. Reviewing the album in 2000 for PopMatters, Devon Powers called it "camp" and "a caricature of herself." But in the early 2000s, I was deeply entrenched in the aesthetic of pop music, where *NSYNC and Britney could be camp and larger than life. It's no surprise, then, that the summer I became obsessed with Britney Spears and S Club 7, I was also obsessed with this incarnation of Lil' Kim.

When I thought of rap music, I thought of Biggie and 2Pac and men talking about bitches they fucked and enemies they shot and lobbing "faggot" at one another as an insult. Witnessing Lil' Kim rapping over a Latin sample ("Esto Es El Gua-guancó" by Cheo Feliciano) and referencing "Rapper's Delight" made hip-hop seem fun and buoyant and every bit as aspirational as a Britney Spears video where she dresses up in a skin-tight red catsuit. I didn't know that choreography existed in rap music, so in seeing Kim in designer boots, a crimped blond wig, panties, and a corset, I thought she seemed like a growner, sexier version of what Spears had been selling in her videos and on that *Rolling Stone* cover.

The album dropped the weekend I arrived in Vegas, and I bought it on my first visit to that nearby Tower Records. When I got back to my papaw's condo, I was immediately met with one of the raunchiest albums I'd ever heard, tailor-made to a Milwaukee native with its opening track, touting the line "I may be hardcore, but I'm not Jeffrey Dahmer." The next song opens with a simulation of a woman orgasming, sampled from the 1989 house track "French Kiss" by Lil Louis.

On the track "Suck My Dick," she responds to a man repeatedly calling her a bitch with "Y'all niggas ain't shit, and if I was

a dude, I'd tell you to suck my dick." In the lyrics to "Revolution," she readies an arsenal of weapons ("S-W nine millimeter,
check, long-nose double-barreled rifle, check") while drinking a
Snapple (which used to be a very cunt drink that was served in
a glass bottle and had a cap that literally popped when you
opened it, but now it's sold in plastic bottles, and I can't imagine that's *better* for the environment. Also, they're ugly).

Sisqó joined her on "How Many Licks" as she rapped about
the different dudes she fucked, their dick sizes, and how they
jerked off fantasizing about her. On "Queen Bitch Pt. 2," posthumous vocals from Biggie rap, "You niggas got some audac-
ity. You sold a million, now you're half of me." That was the
first time I'd heard Biggie's vocals and felt any type of gravi-
tational pull toward him aside from on "Hypnotize" or "Mo
Money Mo Problems," but what clearly drew me to those songs
were Pamela Long's vocals on the chorus on the former and
the sample of Diana Ross's "I'm Coming Out" on the latter.

The Notorious K.I.M. was the only CD I scratched up more
than No Strings Attached and Oops! . . . I Did It Again that summer. When I returned to Milwaukee, one Saturday afternoon, I
found myself going through my mom's records to steal her
copy of Aaliyah's One in a Million (I'd become a fan after hearing her two singles off the Romeo Must Die soundtrack), and
that's when I found Lil' Kim's debut album, Hard Core, amid her
collection. On the album cover, Kim is on all fours on a bear-
skin rug, with a bottle of champagne and an assortment of
roses beside her.

I popped it into my CD player and pressed play on the
album for the first time only to discover that the campy, sexually over-the-top Kim from her second album had been spawned
by a much grittier album, Hard Core, released on November 12,
1996, when women were mostly nonexistent in rap. She ex-

uded the sexuality of a porn star, rapping about her pussy and instructing men on how to get her off, while also rapping about guns and drugs with as much intensity as her male counterparts, like Biggie and the rest of Junior M.A.F.I.A.

The album opens with a skit where a man hops out of a New York City cab and buys a movie ticket: "One for Lil' Kim. *Hard Core.*" He then purchases a small popcorn, a large order of butter, and a bunch of napkins. When he sits in his seat, you can hear simulated sex, and you realize he's watching a porn flick starring Kim. It's followed by the sound of him unzipping his pants and loudly jerking off, presumably using the butter as lube. He moans, "Kim . . . Kim . . . Yeah . . . Work it, bitch!" and then you're immediately thrust into the track "Big Momma Thang," where Kim boasts, in her first lines on the album, "I used to be scared of the dick. Now I throw lips to the shit, handle it like a real bitch!"

Nothing could prepare me for hearing that for the first time. Up till then, I hadn't even publicly acknowledged being gay. I hadn't even discovered real gay porn yet; I'd only ever looked at photos of naked men on search engines. The raunchiest thing my mom had found on her computer at that point was a *Buffy* fanfic I'd been reading called "The First Time" where Buffy and Giles had sex (disgusting in retrospect, but the prose was *very* explicit and turned me on as a thirteen-year-old).

Kim, to me, felt like she had opened an entire new realm of possibilities not only in the type of music I listened to, but also in expressing a sexuality that did not involve "fucking bitches" like the men my mom listened to while she drove me to school, or like my classmates claimed they did on the weekend whenever we sat in homeroom on a Monday morning. In an interview with bell hooks for *Paper* in 1997, hooks didn't find the entire Pussy Galore persona of Kim that novel, writing, "The only new thing happening here is that it took so long for a hip-hop girl to make the down-and-dirty talk pay her bills big-time. Mark my words. Long before Lil' Kim could speak, smart sluts of all ages were talking trash. To talk trash and get paid has always been harder for women than for men. This 21-year-old has gone where others have not been able to go, 'cause she's got the right dudes behind her."

But for a kid who didn't grow up in New York but instead Milwaukee, I had never seen "smart sluts" and had certainly never heard women talking trash like this. If they did, it was definitely when I was put to bed and my mom and aunts would start pouring the liquor and playing spades. It was an introduction to sex, the type of sex that involved men, that involved dicks. The very kind that I was continuously searching for on the internet. Of the album's lyrical content, hooks asks Kim:

> BELL HOOKS: What was your line on *Hard Core*, "Take it up the butt"? Don't be funnin'. What do you think about that?
>
> LIL' KIM: I think it's real.
>
> BELL HOOKS: Tell me what you mean when you say it's real—that a lot of people are getting fucked in the butt?
>
> LIL' KIM: Exactly. I mean, there are a lot of women out there who are doing crazy things behind closed doors sexual-wise and are afraid to admit it. And I'm like, "Yeah, I take it in the butt. That's right. Whatever."

Kim was really *that* bitch. And it was her frankness about anal sex in a conversation with bell hooks in 1997 that made it less weird for me when I discovered my first porn sites, like

Sean Cody and BiLatinMen. Typically, whenever kids at school made jokes about being gay, they'd reference someone being fucked in the ass. I mean, damn, the first time I'd ever witnessed anal sex on film, it was in 1994's *Pulp Fiction*, where Ving Rhames is raped in a back room. But here was Kim rapping "take it up the butt" like it was no big deal to her. Because it wasn't. She just wanted to get off.

Up until then, I'd grown up finding most sexual things to be bad. I had to hide the fact that I wasn't into girls. I had to sneak watching gay porn on the computer when everyone else was asleep. Even my favorite TV show, *Buffy*, indoctrinated me with sex as a sin. Though in essence, the show was a repudiation of the blond girl with nice tits who gets murdered that littered most slasher and other horror films, when Buffy has sex for the first time with her boyfriend Angel (a good vampire with a soul), he loses his soul and turns into a blood-lusting killing machine.

When I watched *Buffy* as a teenager, the conservative journey of her sexuality never seemed odd to me. But as an adult who rewatches my favorite show a few times a year, I wish that Buffy felt better about her sex life. She has sex with her first boyfriend, and he turns evil. The second time she has sex, in college with a guy named Parker, he treats her like dirt. She dates an extremely boring man like Riley, and I guess the sex is good, but if that is supposed to be an aspirational relationship, then, really, we were all doomed.

It wasn't until Buffy started having sex with Spike, a "bad" vampire who didn't have a soul but a chip in his brain that prevented him from harming humans, that she really seemed to not only enjoy sex, but also experiment with different positions, fetishes like light bondage, and yes, anal sex. During one episode where she and Spike have sex on the balcony of the night-club the Bronze, it's heavily implied that they're having anal sex. And she's made to feel ashamed of it.

Buffy and Spike's relationship starts off volatile; after all, he was one of her greatest foes before they developed feelings for each other. When they first have sex, in the episode "Smashed," their passion erupts in a drawn-out fight that tears down the very foundation of the abandoned house they're fighting in. But afterward, something odd happens: Buffy, struggling with the loss of her mother, newfound adult responsibilities, and a lingering depression from being brought back from the dead, somehow manages to laugh. The moments when she enjoys her relationship with Spike are truly sublime in an otherwise-emotionally dreary season.

But in that anal-sex moment, writer Steven S. DeKnight's script describes her as "wracked with guilt." But would this have seemed out of place in *Fifty Shades of Grey*? On *Sex and the City*, Miranda was already enjoying the thrills of public sex, and George Michael was making tongue-in-cheek references to his "lewd behavior" arrest in his 1998 single "Outside." As a teenager, I felt that shame right alongside Buffy, but as an adult, I can't lie that I find the moment exhilarating and wonder why it was even written if it only exists to shame our heroine. It seems like it was, because Buffy is punished for her relationship with Spike with him attempting to rape her later in the season.

Throughout the season she hasn't confided in her friends about her sex life, and then it all comes back to haunt her. And I wonder why I have always felt uneasy confiding about my own sex life with my friends, sometimes even to this day. I always ask myself, was it because the act felt sinful to me? Or was it that I didn't even see myself as an object of sexual desire, and so I felt embarrassed talking about any sexual encounter I'd had or wished I'd had with any of my gay friends, who all seemed to have much more active sex lives than my own?

As much as *Hard Core* rewired my brain for what was possible, a month later I was at Marquette, an all-boys school, where I felt like I had to retreat deeper into the closet—after all, people already made jokes about everyone at the school being a faggot. So I listened to Lil' Kim and Britney Spears on my Discman at school, but I made sure to keep the volume low. I couldn't let anyone hear me listen to a woman rapping about *dick*, of all things.

A few years after the interview with Kim, bell hooks wrote her 2002 book of essays, *Rock My Soul: Black People and Self-Esteem*, and remarked on how far Lil' Kim had come in the years since she'd interviewed her after *Hard Core*. She writes, "In black youth culture white supremacist aesthetics prevail. Yet they are given their most graphic expression in representations of the black female. While black male rappers create anti-racist lyrics that project critical consciousness, that consciousness stops when it comes to the black female body. Dark-skinned females are rarely depicted at all. And even light-skinned black females get no play unless they have long straight hair." The "critical consciousness" line veers a bit into placing respectability politics on Lil' Kim, but as with most bell hooks essays, you take what works for you and keep it pushing.

Largely, hooks was commenting on Kim becoming significantly lighter in complexion and adorning herself in blond wigs around the time *The Notorious K.I.M.* dropped. After all, the Lil' Kim of *Hard Core* wouldn't get to appear on *TRL* debuting her video to a horde of screaming white teenagers. But the Lil' Kim of *The Notorious K.I.M.* could. In a 2000 *Newsweek* interview,

Kim remarked on this: "I have low self-esteem—I always have. Guys have always cheated on me with women who were European-looking. You know, the long-hair type. Really beautiful women that left me thinking, 'How can I compete with that?' Being a regular Black girl wasn't good enough."

Lil' Kim has always said that her rap persona helped her deal with her insecurities better, in that she got to dress up in expensive clothes and look like a movie star. This was the "camp" Kim was leaning into, as Powers remarked in her 2000 review of *The Notorious K.I.M.*, which hooks referred to as "[distorting] her natural beauty to become a cartoonlike caricature of whiteness" to bolster her success.

It's a sad irony that the very thing that made Kim more accessible to audiences, which led me to her because I was on a diet of white pop-culture media in a rejection of my mother, was the thing that tortured her self-esteem and how she viewed herself. Attending Marquette, I would be surrounded by white boys who were very much the "all-American" ideal, the kind of boys who could stand outside of an Abercrombie & Fitch at the mall, shirtless, to sell teenagers jeans and polo shirts, which beat down my self-esteem. But for about an hour every day, when I listened to Kim in my headphones, I could pray for the day when I, too, wouldn't be scared.

You ain't gotta be rich, but fuck that. How we gonna get
around on your bus pass?

—AMIL, "CAN I GET A . . ." (1998)

· · · · ·

A VIRGIN WHO CAN'T DRIVE

February 2, 1999, marked the release of the most important
historical text since the Bible[*]: "A scrub is a guy that can't
get no love from me, hanging out the passenger side of his best
friend's ride, trying to holla at me." TLC's "No Scrubs" was
seminal for me (the version with Left Eye's rap only), not because it was a massive hit, but because my mom and sister routinely lobbed the lyrics at me over the fact that I never got my
driver's license in high school.

For most teenagers, a car represents freedom. For instance,
my younger sister got her driver's permit as soon as she could.
But for me, who had a life that revolved around watching TV
and walking to the comic book store and going to the movies
at the mall, there didn't seem to be much of a need to get my
license. Besides, driver's ed seemed to happen immediately
after school, and that coincided with rehearsals for the school
plays. I worked on the stage crew for each show, because I was
finding myself falling in love with theater more and more, and
if I couldn't be cast in a show, then I'd at least take a job that
would let me take part in all the magic that I dreamed about

---

[*] The Bible of course being the print edition of *Entertainment Weekly* (February
1990–April 2022).

when I would listen to the *Rent* original Broadway cast recording in my bedroom and try to make my high-pitched gay voice deep enough to match Adam Pascal's raspy voice on "Another Day."

Oddly enough, I have always thought I had a high-pitched gay voice, another one of the "giveaways" that I lived in fear of every time I had to speak in class or answer the phone and someone thought it was my mother on the other end. But I now realize there were multiple things going on there. For one, whenever I answered the phone, I would immediately code-switch, like I'd learned to from my mom. I spoke in a more relaxed manner around my family, but on the phone, I mimicked my mom's professional, high-pitched, friendly white-woman voice that would often get people to do things for you.

Although sometimes my gay voice just read as a white voice to people at school. If it weren't enough that I was worried I sounded gay, I was also worried about sounding white. Multiple people made fun of my voice as a kid. It didn't have much to do with my vocabulary words or the fact that I liked to read that made me seem "white" to my classmates; it was my speech. I mean, I had horrible grades, so no one would ever accuse me of trying to be "better" than anyone else in our grade.

But my little gay voice combined with the fact that I lived with my grandmother and my sister lived with my mother, meaning my sister was the one who developed much more AAVE (African American Vernacular English) in her vocabulary, always made me feel self-conscious about how I sound. Ironically, now that speaking is sort of my regular job as the host of a podcast, I hear from people all the time about how much they love my voice or how deep it sounds. Some puberty hit between then and now, but even so, my voice still sounds high-pitched to *me*, and I still can't stand the sound of it. To me, everyone could tell something about me just by me opening my mouth.

Honestly, with all the white-teen-girl media I consumed from the WB—*Buffy* to *Felicity* to *Dawson's Creek* to *Charmed**—I did feel a bit like *Clueless*'s Dionne, a bougie Black girl played by Stacey Dash who understands the ins and outs of white culture and whose best friend is rich white Beverly Hills teenager Alicia Silverstone's Cher Horowitz.

The teen comedy, based on Jane Austen's 1815 English-society novel, *Emma*, was released in 1995 and written and directed by Amy Heckerling. It stars Alicia Silverstone as Cher, a rich, sometimes vain, and ditzy teenager. It was probably the defining teen movie of the nineties, and *Clueless*'s Cher and her best friend, Dionne, are pop-culture staples: There'll never be another Halloween in recorded human history where someone *doesn't* dress up as the two friends. Dionne speaks like a white L.A. girl most of the time, but it's easy to imagine she code-switches at home or in private with her boyfriend, Murray (Donald Faison).

At my high school, I was surrounded by multiple rich white kids, but there weren't any Dionnes. At times, though, I tried to carry myself like I was her, because even the air of bougieness, acting like you're above certain things, can at least make *you* feel like you were born into a different social status in life. In

---

* Mom and I both loved *Charmed*, and we both loved the toxic relationship between Phoebe and the demon Cole, which, in retrospect, seems like fore-shadowing of my adult romantic life.

reality, all it kind of did was make me seem self-centered and vain to some of my classmates (and probably puzzling, because I definitely did not have any kind of status or money to back it up).

In retrospect, becoming hypercritical of people's fashion and music tastes was probably another dead giveaway that I was a homo, much like Christian, the boy Cher tries dating in *Clueless* who loves shopping, just like her, and listening to Billie Holiday, only for Cher to discover, as Murray observes in one of the scene's funniest lines, "he's a disco-dancing, Oscar Wilde–reading, Streisand-ticket-holding friend of Dorothy, know what I'm saying?"

Never mind why Murray himself knows so many markers of what being a faggot is. None of these really applied to me besides the disco dancing, if only because one of the few episodes of *The Simpsons* I'd managed to see in syndication was "Homer's Phobia," where Homer realizes his new friend, John, is gay after he listens to records like Alicia Bridges's 1978 disco single "I Love the Nightlife (Disco 'Round)." But I wouldn't even discover Oscar Wilde until I read *The Importance of Being Earnest* in college. I suppose I did love *The Wizard of Oz*, but I'd always preferred *The Wiz*.

Cher Horowitz and I were both virgins who couldn't drive. One of the more famous scenes in *Clueless* involves Dionne attempting to drive on the freeway in Los Angeles and nearly dying—which would also happen to me years later when I finally got my driver's license and moved to Los Angeles. I guess Bret Easton Ellis was right in *Less than Zero* when he opened the novel with "People are afraid to merge on freeways in Los

Angeles."* In lieu of driving, I became very familiar with the Milwaukee transit system. All the independence I needed was the ability to take the bus from my gran's house directly to Mayfair on the weekends when I wanted to catch a movie. And I could take the bus to school, even if it involved two buses (the 66 and the 30, usually), with no problem. I had no real incentive to need to drive.

At least, that's what I assumed as a high school freshman. The first time I remember catching a ride from a friend at school, it was after the cast and crew went to Denny's after a show. Denny's as a post-show ritual is common to most American theater kids who didn't live in small towns with a local diner. The Denny's menus were large, plastic-wrapped like my aunt Ruth's sofa that I sweated on while watching *The Price Is Right* and a marathon of CBS soap operas with her on summer days, and it had pictures of all the food items on the page so you knew what you were getting.

By my high school years, the menus were more professional than the Denny's menus I remembered as a kid, which were Jetsons- or Flintstones-themed. In part because I don't know that either of those animated Hanna-Barbera franchises have any continued pop-culture relevance post the release of 2000's *The Flintstones in Viva Rock Vegas*, a movie with a higher critical rating than its 1994 predecessor *The Flintstones*, but also a sequel that no one remembers aside from its goofy title because the original film's cast (John Goodman, Rick Moranis, Eliza-

---

* One of my favorite novels. And, actually, aside from *Imperial Bedrooms*, a misguided sequel to *Less than Zero*, I'm a fan of everything Ellis has written—if I pretend that it was all a drug-addled dream that during the Trump administration he wrote a memoir called *White*, presumably about being white. I wouldn't know, seeing as how it never happened!

beth Perkins, and Rosie O'Donnell, with Kyle MacLachlan and Halle Berry in supporting roles) are all absent from the sequel (technically a prequel, starring Mark Addy,* Stephen Baldwin, Kristen Johnston, and Jane Krakowski, with Alan Cumming and Joan Collins in supporting roles, the only iconic part of the film).

Much like *Looney Tunes*, *The Flintstones* and *The Jetsons* are cartoons that most millennials grew up with because they were always in syndication and their parents loved them. As a kid, I rewatched 1990's *Jetsons: The Movie* as much as I watched any Disney film (and listened to its banger soundtrack with Tiffany songs, probably the only Tiffany songs I knew as a kid). Nowadays, the only Hanna-Barbera franchise that anyone under millennial age remembers is Scooby-Doo, which is in part due to the James Gunn film franchise from the 2000s, continued reboots of the franchise, and the fact that Shaggy's stoner vibes and the queerness of Fred and Velma have continued to make them relevant to younger audiences, whereas *The Jetsons* has weird, outdated gender roles and *The Flintstones* has the original Jar Jar Binks† in it, the Great Gazoo.

Until I'd reached high school, I kinda had no idea that there were so many white people in Wisconsin. I got picked up by my gran at Denny's because no one else lived near me, and

---

* Addy became famous after his film debut in *The Full Monty*, a 1997 film that gained popularity because it's about steelworkers who become male strippers. An actual good film (and then a great musical), it's the inverse of *Flashdance*, an awful film about a female steelworker turned dancer.

† People have tried to create retrospective support for Jar Jar Binks, arguing he was maligned by adults who watched the Star Wars prequels when he's no different from R2-D2 or C-3PO. But those are robots. And Jar Jar is a jive-talking weirdo. I hate him. Honestly, though, I love the first two prequel movies. I think 2019's *The Rise of Skywalker* has shown that if anything, Star Wars trilogies in general suffer from horrible third films.

that's when I realized another large difference between me and the kids at Marquette: Very few of them lived in *Milwaukee*. They lived in the *county* of Milwaukee, which includes villages Brown Deer, Fox Point, and Whitefish Bay, or neighboring cities, like Brookfield, Mequon, Port Washington, and Oconomowoc.

The city of Milwaukee was heavily diverse and every school I'd attended until high school was too. Whenever I saw white people in public, I had no idea where they lived. As a child, I was not aware of the existence of the suburbs. This is a complete contrast to how most people outside of Wisconsin view Milwaukee. Sitcoms like *Happy Days* have still dominated pop culture with the notion that Milwaukee is a very white city, like it was in the fifties.

In the 1900s, Milwaukee had a higher percentage of foreign-born residents than any city in the United States. According to Reggie Jackson in *Milwaukee Independent*, "More than 4 million Italians arrived from 1890 through 1920. Over 2 million Jews escaping the pogroms in Eastern Europe arrived between 1880 and 1920. Nearly 1.5 million immigrants arrived in 1907, the largest number for any year. Many of these newly arriving immigrants arrived in big cities like Chicago, Detroit, New York, Philadelphia, and Milwaukee." Then came Black people, who escaped the lynchings and other prejudices of the Jim Crow South by migrating north to the cities that the railroad tracks (real railroads, not Miss Harriet's) led them directly to, like Detroit, Chicago, Cleveland, and Milwaukee.

Within ten years, from 1940 to 1950, the U.S. Census shows the Black population of Milwaukee nearly tripling. Anti-immigrant and anti-Black sentiment led to white flight, the term used to describe white people moving in droves out of American cities and into the suburbs, which became white enclaves using housing discrimination, police discrimination, and other racist tactics to keep Black people out of the suburbs. When those didn't work, they just borrowed some shit from the South and burned down Black homes and businesses and lynched niggas too.

Despite the assumption that only Southern states like to teach science fiction when it comes to U.S. history, most Northern states make it a point not to include the Northern race riots in their history lessons. It's why so many Americans didn't learn about the Tulsa massacre until they watched HBO's adaptation of *Watchmen* in 2019, or about the 12th Street Riot in Detroit until it was depicted in Kathryn Bigelow's 2017 film *Detroit.** I certainly was never taught a course on the long, hot summer of 1967, in which the 12th Street Riot and over a hundred other race riots occurred in American cities. That summer included the 1967 Milwaukee riot, which in turn led to Milwaukee becoming the most racially segregated city in America. My family had moved to the north from Tiptonville, Tennessee, and white people wanted *out*, okay?

As I began to make friends at Marquette, it became more apparent that the barrier to me hanging out with friends after school was a car, but for the most part, I still had all of the socializing I could take by being involved in theater, and summers I usually spent by myself, engrossed in comics and TV and film. I am not *not* calling myself dumb, but because I never investigated the concept of taking driver's ed, and my family usually left me to my devices, no one ever told me that it was possible to take driver's ed during the summer or outside of the driver's ed classes that Marquette offered after school, which were of

---

* Depicted horribly, mind you. Not to sound like a Fox News anchor, but let's stay *out* of the politics and get back to making films about surfers who rob banks (*Point Break*) or Angela Bassett sci-fi thrillers (*Strange Days*).

course when we would rehearse for plays, so I never bothered to take them.

And as a person who struggled making friends anyway, one thing that made me closer to friends of mine was my Drew Barrymore life of riding in cars with boys (without the teen pregnancy, of course). By becoming known as the person who needed a ride all the time, I developed closer friendships with a few people in the class because they became my go-to after-school or post-party rides. Some of my favorite moments were catching a ride with someone from school I barely knew, like the time a bunch of kids in class went to see the movie *Miracle* and I rode with several kids on the hockey team and heard the J-Kwon song "Tipsy" for the first time as they rapped along to it.

Or the time my friend Cliff drove me across town from school to a birthday party on the Lower East Side of Milwaukee at Pizza Shuttle (the best pizza I've had outside of New York, which I guess makes some sort of weird sense because it's located in a neighborhood with a New York name, and much like NY's Lower East Side, it's crawling with drunk college students). During the ride we listened to the Strokes' entire second album, *Room on Fire*, which I'd mostly listened to on my own at home after falling in love with Roman Coppola's music video for the single "12:51." I had no idea that anyone else at school even liked the Strokes until the drive with Cliff, and that one car ride, singing aloud to "Under Control," helped make *Room on Fire* one of the most important albums of my teenage years.

On the occasions that I couldn't get a ride home because the person I was counting on for a ride didn't want to drive in the direction of my house, Gran would pick me up. One time, during a cast party that raged on too long, I was stuck at a house in Brookfield and my gran was asleep and the buses had long stopped running, because the buses don't run that late at night into the white parts of town, if they run there at all. So, in one of my more embarrassing moments, I had to pretend to be asleep in the corner of the basement where all of the straight kids were as they were all making out with their girlfriends in their sleeping bags.

But for the most part, my best friends Luke and Andy were the ones who dropped me off at home whenever I deigned to be social, but I do remember that the majority of my rides in school were from Derek, a kid who was part of my extended theater-and-art-kid friend group, who I was friends with but not close friends with, and I only ever had conversations with him while he was driving me home. But some of my favorite convos about movies and TV shows I loved happened during drives with Derek.

At a certain point I did have to pretend that I *had* a license but that I never had a car to use. This came back to bite me in the ass once (because one thing about those tables is that they turn!) during a rehearsal when my friend Matt asked me to move his car for him. After seven p.m., students had to move their cars to the street and out of the student parking lot. Because Matt and everyone else believed I *did* have a license, and he was stage manager, he asked me to move his car and there was no other option of getting anyone else to do it, and the only *other* option was admitting to everyone that I'd been lying about having a driver's license.

In retrospect, telling the truth about the license was probably the better option than deciding I'd been in enough cars with people to figure out how to move a car. I took Matt's keys, a ball of anxiety as I trekked to the student lot and climbed into his car and started the engine, and then I put the car in reverse and pressed the gas pedal and slammed into a wall. The school's security guard found me and asked me what happened, and I claimed I had a migraine that accidentally caused me to hit the gas.

He asked for my license, and I said that I'd forgotten it at home, and when he *pressed* me about whether I really had a license, like he could tell I was lying—and he probably could, because a close friend randomly told me when we were on ketamine at a house party at around four a.m. that he knew I could never be a sociopath like a lot of people he'd encountered in L.A. because I'm a notoriously bad liar. I told the security guard that I had my *permit*, not my license, and he demanded that I bring it to school the next day, and I promised Matt that this was also the truth. Eventually, Matt confronted me when he realized that I did not have a license, and I admitted everything, and he looked at me like I was the dumbest person he'd ever met (probably true) and said, "You could've just said you didn't have a license. Who cares?"

This was my first lesson in the fact that most of the anxieties and dramatic situations that pop into my head have no real basis in reality, which probably is what makes me a writer but also makes me an exhausting person to be friends with.

That was one of the four big lies I told in high school. The second one, obviously, was the gay one. The third was the time I discovered a credit card in the drawer of my gran's apartment and used it as my own personal credit card for a year in high school without telling her, because I didn't really know how credit cards worked or how they were paid off, and a bill never seemed to arrive at the house, so that certainly didn't encourage me to *stop* using it. This was the year that I started primarily shopping at the Buckle, a "cool" clothing store at the mall that let me finally wear jeans that weren't from Kohl's or JCPenney, and it seemed like my family had come into money.

I also purchased a brown suede jacket from the Buckle that became my favorite article of clothing, mostly because I could wear it in school over my required collared shirts (at least, when I could avoid the two teachers who made me take it off), which, to me, was a way of hiding the fat in my body that protruded from tight-fitting polo shirts. I used this card to purchase my first gay porn DVD, *The Hole*, a porn parody of *The Ring* that revealed I was gay when my gran found it in my bedroom.

And then the fourth lie I told was about where I was accepted to college.

When it came time to apply to colleges, I only had one in mind—New York University. I loved the idea of moving to New York and doing theater and being an artist like those broke characters in *Rent*, plus I'd overheard Kevin, my friend I'd had a crush on all four years of school, talking about applying to NYU. Unfortunately for me, my school guidance counselor thought that the idea of me going to NYU was laughable, probably because of my grades, but also because she was kind of rude and didn't take my interest in theater or going to Tisch seriously.

At any rate, NYU was far too expensive for anyone in my family to afford. Also, 9/11 had just happened, and people in Milwaukee seemed very concerned that the city was a terrorism hot spot. So my two options for colleges I could reasonably get into were two Jesuit colleges, much like MUHS. One was, obviously, Marquette University, which practically anyone from MUHS could get into, and the second was Loyola University Chicago. I had applied to DePaul and Columbia College, two other Chicago schools with good theater programs, and been denied, so maybe my rude counselor was right about NYU after all! I got into both Marquette and Loyola, but only Marquette offered me nearly a full ride, and I would have had to take out loans if I attended Loyola.

Faced with the option of having to feel like I was still at home, going to college with people I'd gone to high school with, I finally had my moment of wanting freedom that most teenagers experience when they get their driver's license. And then there was Loyola, in a city that felt like New York, where my gay uncle had once lived, with a public transportation system that didn't even require me to have a car.

I shredded my acceptance to Marquette and told my gran that I'd been rejected and the only school I'd gotten into was Loyola. She was disappointed. I know she was hoping I'd stay in Milwaukee, but I wanted to escape my hometown and start a real life, any kind of different life. "I never really thought you'd stay in this city," a friend from high school told me when I ran into them years later. So, thanks to my fourth big lie, I was heading to Chicago.

Oh, it's already been broughten!

—PRISCILLA, *NOT ANOTHER TEEN MOVIE* (2001)

· · · · ·

BRING IT

Once upon a time, my favorite movie was the 2001 Baz Luhrmann film *Moulin Rouge!*, a romantic musical starring Nicole Kidman and Ewan McGregor where McGregor plays a down-on-his-luck poet in love with Kidman's Satine, a dancer and prostitute who works at the famed Moulin Rouge, a cabaret in Paris that has existed since 1889 and now shows up in blurry photos that straight couples post to Instagram.

It's no wonder why the musical fantasy was my favorite film—it was preceded by "Lady Marmalade," a massive pop single on its soundtrack and cover of the 1974 disco song from Patti Labelle. This version repurposed the famous line "Voulez-vous coucher avec moi, ce soir?" which translates to "Do you want to sleep with me?" and is the only French phrase that most Americans know. The 2001 version featured Christina Aguilera, Mýa, Pink, and Lil' Kim and forever launched karaoke fights among gay men over who gets to perform as Aguilera or Kim and who will be forced to sing Mýa's part (I do love Mýa, but unfortunately not wanting to sing her part holds true for "Cell Block Tango" from *Chicago* as well, which Mýa is also a part of . . . She's great, but hers are the least fun verses in each song).

My love of Luhrmann films tends to wane after the immediate spectacle of it all, and what I really appreciate most is the music above all else, except in *Australia*, which is awful, and *Elvis*, which is a masterpiece. But my love of *Moulin Rouge!* has never wavered since the summer of 2001, when I watched it again and again at the movies. It's the film that fueled my love of Nicole Kidman. It seems odd to love Kidman as much as I love Tom Cruise, but their larger-than-life personas on- and off-screen make them today's most lasting and essential movie *stars*, save for Will Smith.

In all honesty, I have no recollection of Cruise and Kidman as a married couple. In high school, I was into films but not celebrity gossip—that interest wouldn't even truly develop until I got my first magazine job at *Radar* when I moved to New York. I was also far too young to have any real interest in *Eyes Wide Shut* when it was released in 1999, so I hadn't even seen them on-screen together, nor did I know the magic of Stanley Kubrick. I'd seen *The Shining*, of course, but didn't discover a love for Kubrick's films until a midnight screening of *2001: A Space Odyssey* one summer after high school.

As with most of the actresses I love dearly, I first discovered Nicole Kidman in a supporting role in an action film—*Batman Forever*—where she plays Dr. Chase Meridian (the Batman franchise has given me so much. It's also where I first fell in love with Michelle Pfeiffer via *Batman Returns**)—which is a reason I'm an advocate for prestige actors appearing in comic book films. Film snobs and white gay men who stan actresses on the internet tend to hate this, but that's where burgeoning young gays are going to discover their future favorite character actresses and Oscar-winning divas. They would have you believe

---

* Michelle Pfeiffer was nominated for Best Actress at the 1993 Oscars for her role in *Love Field*, but she should've been nominated for *Batman Returns* that year. And she should've won.

that ten-year-olds are sitting down to watch *Malice* or *To Die For*, but no, they're discovering their future Nicole Kidman from movies like *Batman Forever* and *The Peacemaker* (a dumb movie whose only relevant place in pop culture is that it spurred rumors that Kidman and her co-star George Clooney were having an affair amid her Cruise divorce).

I bought the *Moulin Rouge!* two-disc DVD box set the instant it appeared at Sam Goody and watched it religiously every weekend. I became an obsessive stan of the film. I even listened to the soundtrack every day on the way to school, having multiple daydreams about performing "El Tango de Roxanne" in our school auditorium before the entire student body. I often had fantasies of performing on that stage that had never been realized, so when Satine and McGregor as Christian slip into their fantastical worlds full of song and dance, it felt a lot like how my imagination buzzed every time I listened to music, particularly the music of the shows our school performed for our spring musicals.

To this day, our production of *Guys and Dolls* is why it's one of my favorite musicals, alongside *West Side Story*, *Footloose*, and the extremely bizarre *Crazy for You*, which Frankensteins together a bunch of Gershwin songs from the 1930 musical *Girl Crazy* and a bunch of other productions to make a new musical in 1992. If I had a longing to be in one of our school's musicals, destined to audition for each of them and yet never be cast in any, then the diametric opposite was my friend Sawyer. Sawyer, whose only fault seemed to be that he was Tom Cruise's height, was not only our student government president, but he also managed to be handsome, charismatic, a good dancer, and a very good singer.

Ms. Halston and Father Wilkinson couldn't wait to boo me

off the audition stage like we were at the Apollo, but they absolutely couldn't wait for Sawyer to audition for every show, musical or otherwise. To paraphrase Aja speaking to Valentina on *RuPaul's Drag Race*, Sawyer was perfect, he was beautiful, he looked like Linda Evangelista, he was a model. You would not be surprised to know that Sawyer was my high school nemesis. But it wasn't because he got cast in every fucking school play while I was relegated to skulking in the shadows with the rest of the stage crew like the fucking Phantom of the Opera. No, it was because Sawyer borrowed my *Moulin Rouge!* DVD. And then he lost it.

I'm a person who has always enjoyed having a nemesis. A rival. An adversary. There's a reason all stories since the creation of mankind have involved a protagonist and an antagonist. And a rivalry is the point of the best film ever made: *Bring It On.*

The 2000 film starring Kirsten Dunst and Gabrielle Union is a comedy about idiotic teenage white cheerleaders who steal cheers from Black, underprivileged cheerleaders in Compton. It's the film I've seen the most in theaters, no fewer than six times, which had less to do with my love of the film and more with the fact that it was released in late August, before my first semester of high school, and that the next film of any interest to me to be released would be *Remember the Titans* in late September, so I spent every weekend rewatching *Bring It On* for an entire month. This isn't to say no good films were released then, but I was fourteen at the time and did not discover my love of other films released in the fall of 2000 like *Nurse Betty* or *Almost Famous* until years later. Iconic horror sequel *Urban Legends: Final Cut* was also released in this time frame, but as with most horror movies I watched as a teenager, it was via a bootleg DVD from the barbershop. A month is a long time when you're a teenager, and you often find that you can fill your after-noons watching multiple films at the mall.

Bring It On, made on a budget of about ten million dollars, grossed over ninety million dollars at the box office and has grown into one of the fondly remembered teen movies of the 2000s. At the time, Roger Ebert in the *Chicago Sun-Times* called the film "yet another example of the most depressing trend of the summer of 2000, the cynical attempt by Hollywood to cram R-rated material into PG-13-rated movies. This is done not to corrupt our children, but (even worse) with complete indifference to their developing values. The real reason is more cynical: Younger teenagers buy a lot of tickets and are crucial if a movie hopes to 'win the weekend.' The R-rating is a penalty at the box office.

"So, movies that were born to be R, like *Gone in 60 Seconds*, *Coyote Ugly* and *Bring It On*, are trimmed to within a millimeter of the dividing line and released as PG-13, so that any child tall enough to push dollars through the ticket window is cheerfully admitted, with or without an adult." At the time, *Bring It On* was seen as a crass, hypersexualized film marketed to kids. Ironically, current rated-R comedies like the recent Jennifer Lawrence vehicle *No Hard Feelings* seem less raunchy than teen films of the 2000s.

In an era where teenagers actually spent money at the mov-ies and would quote the crude sex jokes they heard to their friends, it made sense. Looking back on it now, the movie feels like it's from a completely different time—there's little chance a PG-13 film would get away with liberal use of the words "fag" or "retarded"* in their jokes today. The Puritanification

---

* Though the Black Eyed Peas *did* have a pretty large hit titled "Let's Get It Started," for which the album version was titled "Let's Get Retarded." The

of America has managed to make *Bring It On* edgier than it was in 2000 (at least most of the jokes are repeatable, unlike any of the films in the Scary Movie franchise, which even horrified me on a recent rewatch).

A sequel has been teased multiple times, but I fear that the chances about as dismal as a sequel to the 2010 Angelina Jolie film *Salt*, for which I have been running a grassroots campaign for about fourteen years. Angelina Jolie should be making as many action films as Tom Cruise still does, but whereas Cruise only cares about saving the world on film, Jolie seems interested in saving the actual world we live in. Which is all well and good, but I desperately need to see her don more bad wigs and kill Russian spies—who cares about actual human rights laws?

Ebert wasn't wrong, though his tirade that *Bring It On* was "peddling smut to children" seems a bit aggressive, even for the time. None of the jokes in the film felt particularly *shocking* to me as a fourteen-year-old, mostly because the 2000s were already crass. We were watching *Undressed* on MTV in the middle of the night. We were watching *Jerry Springer* in the afternoon. The fact that when I mention the film *Bring It On* to people my age they usually respond gushingly about the film even if they haven't seen it since high school shows that for most millennials the film represented our sense of humor at the time. And the fact that there were actual gay characters in the film (and one probably bi character) who aren't the butt of horrifically homophobic jokes (I emphasize the "horrific"

---

song was available on streaming platforms till about 2021, and I genuinely believe the only reason it was removed was because COVID lockdowns gathered a lot of millennials together to party with their close friends, which resulted in them making playlists mostly of the music they all grew up listening to. Around 2020, there was a large uptick online of people rediscovering this song's existence and, well, that was the end of that.

because while there are homophobic characters in the film, the jokes themselves are all funny) made the film feel and still seem more progressive than others at the time.

And then there's the East Compton Clovers, the competent cheerleaders, the ones with charisma, uniqueness, nerve, and talent. The Toros steal the Clovers' routines for years until Gabrielle Union's Isis (unfortunate name. I'm thankful the film was not released a year later or it might not be a classic) puts her foot down and declares that her team is going to compete at Nationals and get what's rightfully been denied to them. What might seem to be a frivolous cheerleading movie is one of the only good films about cultural appropriation that's ever been made and most certainly one of the best films about race in America.

It might be hard to remember this because *Bring It On* was released during a time of particularly shitty teen movies about race. First, there's the adaptation of Shakespeare's *Othello*, simply titled *O*, which transfers the setting of the play to a high school basketball team. All you need to know is that Mekhi Phifer plays Odin James, the titular *O*, but also his initials are O. J. Like O. J. Simpson. If a movie was ever doing *too* much, it's certainly *O*, but certainly not as much as another film Julia Stiles, who plays the film's Desdemona, stars in.

That would be *Save the Last Dance*. Quite possibly one of the worst films ever made that has survived for far too long in the good graces of nostalgic millennials. The film depicts a white girl, Stiles, whose mom dies, and with that, so does her love of dancing. Until she moves to the South Side of Chicago (the hood, I guess) and falls for a Black boy (Sean Patrick Thomas) who teaches her hip-hop dancing. Along the way, she faces backlash from white people *and* Black people, but she ultimately gets accepted into Juilliard after mixing ballet with hip-hop in her dance audition.

If you were a teenager who watched this film in 2001, when it was released, then you are forgiven for thinking the final dance number was anything short of brilliant. Rewatching it with adult eyes and a developed human brain, you will realize that the dancing is giving suburban mom doing hip-hop dances on TikTok.

The film fails mostly because teen movies about racism are usually bad (another tip for millennials: Do not rewatch *The Color of Friendship*), and most movies about racism are usually bad or overtly sentimental—there are about four good films about race in America. Films about interracial dating are corny, usually, like *Save the Last Dance*, which isn't to say that *all* interracial love stories are bad, only the ones that take place in films about racism. *Far from Heaven* is the only exception I'll make, but it's the lesser adaptation of *All That Heaven Allows*. (*Ali: Fear Eats the Soul* is also an interracial romance but does not involve American racism, so maybe it's only American racism that comes across corny in film.) Most sports films involving Black characters are about race because Hollywood thinks the message of defeating racism is just "triumphing," so those movies, by default, are overly sentimental.

Remember the Titans is saved from being unwatchable schmaltz thanks to Denzel Washington, but it's not particularly *great*. Much better is one of Denzel's best films, *He Got Game*, from Spike Lee, but it's only a sports film that's about Black people, not particularly a film *about* race. Spike Lee is our greatest American director who manages to make films that feel like a depiction of Black lives in America while also not making films about capital-R racism for guilty white audiences to enjoy.

The exceptions to this are *Do the Right Thing* and *Bamboozled*, which are two of the only good films ever made about racism in America (a case can be made for *BlacKkKlansman*, but it's not as good as either of those films and, despite involving the KKK, is more of a thriller than a film that is *about* racism). The third good film about race in America is Douglas Sirk's *Imitation of Life*, a film about a mixed girl who passes for white and rebukes her Black mother (Juanita Moore) until her mother dies and she sobs atop her casket, "I killed my own mother!" Because *Imitation of Life* is a melodrama, it avoids the trap of being overly sentimental because the sentimentality is the objective.

More films about racism should feel over-the-top, have absurdist twists, and be shot in Technicolor. Instead, most of them involve teaching "lessons" about racism. There's nothing to learn about racism in America besides the fact that it exists and sometimes it affects our lives in terrible ways, and even the tears of a white person who has learned the error of their ways can't do much to fix anything.

In theory, the way to make a fantastic film about race in America is not to make a film about race in the first place, and that is why *Bring It On* is the best film made about race in America. It wasn't till I was older that I realized the film puts you in the shoes of Torrance (Kirsten Dunst's character) so you can see exactly why the Clovers deserve to win at the end and why Torrance humbly accepts her team's second-place win. The film weaves in themes of intersectionality, cultural appropriation, and the best ways to dismantle white supremacist power structures.

Sounds like a lot for a raunchy 2000s teen comedy. Still, it's in the moment where Isis turns down money from Torrance's father and instead seeks help from Pauletta, a Black TV host, that you realize it's giving Black *and* white audiences neces-sary tools. For Black audiences, it's a reminder to seek avenues within your own community to prop one another up. For white audiences, it shows that simply throwing money at a problem won't fix a history of injustices. It's only when you level the playing field and truly "bring it" that you see who's the real winner. And in this case, it's the Clovers. Because duh!

Seeing as I couldn't compete with Sawyer when it came to performing, I had to find another way to handle the fact that Sawyer, who had lost my *Moulin Rouge!* DVD, was also the golden boy of MUHS. Aside from being in every school musi-cal, he was also dating a girl from Divine Savior Holy Angels who was also cast in most of our musicals, so here they were, the Tom Cruise and Nicole Kidman of our high school. Not content with being perfect at theater, Sawyer was also elected into our student government and routinely did our morning announcements.

It was like I was slowly being driven crazy with him narrat-ing my school days like Lynne Thigpen on the mic in *The War-riors*, and to make things worse, Sawyer was actually a good friend. I was closeted and awkward, and some part of him seemed to get that, and he was always one of the nicer people to me at school, and we always talked about *Seinfeld* or *Saturday Night Live* episodes (that's all straight kids talked about at school). Maybe I'd taken things too far with thinking of him as my "nemesis." After all, if you have a nemesis in a forest and they don't know you secretly hate them, does the rivalry even exist? I need to work on that metaphor more, but the idea of disliking Sawyer was all very comical. Until he took something *else* from me.

Senior year, I wrote my first play. My friend Luke launched a night called Lo Fi Theatre Night that incorporated original plays and live music and asked me to participate. My first play was some riff on *Days of Our Lives* mixed with a lot of *Who's Afraid of Virginia Woolf?*, about a married couple fighting and one of them shooting the other with a gun, only there's fourth wall breaking, and someone in the audience gets shot with the bullet. So there was probably a lot of sketch comedy sprinkled on it too.

Before that, the only piece of theater I'd worked on was the aforementioned production our school did every fall. The seniors would put on a show called *Follies* where they would parody the school and its teachers. I wish I could take credit for depicting the student government as Nazis with the letter *C* (for Conclave student government) on their armbands and having Sawyer play a version of himself, but I did get a kick out of him realizing we all thought he ruled the student government like a Napoleon Jr. The seniors met every year and decided who wanted to write for *Follies* and who wanted to be in it, and I was on the writing team, where I got to write actual jokes and characters for the first time.

Putting on a show that was going to be produced on the very stage I'd only been allowed on as part of the stage crew, I was finally getting to realize my dreams of being a performer. I wasn't particularly interested in *writing* so much as I was writing a part for myself to be onstage. But the teachers casting *Follies* relegated me to Student #2, which meant that I did spend most of my time coming up with jokes and parody song lyrics (and finding ways to put Student #2 into every scene).

I got the hang of learning choreography, even though my self-consciousness always got the better of me when I danced, because I imagined my large, gay body flailing about beside all the much smaller students I was onstage with. But I was finally feeling like I could be *comfortable* onstage, performing before an auditorium full of people. I was still horrified by public speaking then, so this was kind of a feat. Near the end of rehearsals, it turned out we needed one more song for the show, and I spent all night coming up with lyrics to match the Michael Sembello song "Maniac," which I'd become obsessed with after a night when some of the girls from DSHA introduced us to one of their favorite films, *Flashdance*. *Flashdance* is a horrible film with a great soundtrack and one inspired dance number. Mostly, it's Jennifer Beals in a bad version of *Silkwood*.

When I turned in the song, Ms. Halston was stunned when I said I wanted to sing it myself. It was giving that time a shady-as-hell reporter at the 2008 World Music Awards asked Destiny Child's Michelle Williams, "Oh, *you* sing?"* I insisted that I could sing the damn song. After all, it was mostly chanting anyway. It's not like Michael Sembello is Whitney fucking Houston. But Halston, ever intent on torturing me until I graduated and freed her of my presence, suggested that I audition to sing the song along with the person *she* had in mind: Sawyer. So, I stood there, before her, our musical director, and Sawyer, singing through nerves and warbling out the song like Fergie singing the national anthem. And then Sawyer sang. And he had the voice of a damn angel. But shockingly . . . I got the part! LOL. No, I didn't get the fucking part. Sawyer did. So not only had he lost my *Moulin Rouge!* DVD, but he'd stolen the fucking part I'd written for myself. If I ever had any doubts about Sawyer being my nemesis, they were over.

.   .   .

---

* Michelle Williams has often been slandered as a lesser member of Destiny's Child. Baby, not a *single* person was slacking in Destiny's Child. Except Farrah Franklin.

I've always found a kinship with Ashlee Simpson. On her debut album, *Autobiography*, she has a song titled "Shadow," which is about living in the shadow of the accomplishments of her older sister, Jessica. It gave sister drama for millennials who grew up reading about Elizabeth and Jessica Wakefield constantly sparring in Sweet Valley High. It was hard not to see Ashlee and Jessica pitted against each other all the time. In the early 2000s, Jessica Simpson appeared on *TRL* in rotation with Britney and Christina, but she was never really a serious contender, presented as the religious, girl-next-door alternative to those pop stars.

I mean, she performed at George W. Bush's first inauguration, where she sang her "Jack & Diane"–sampling single "I Think I'm in Love with You," only she replaced the line "Boy, I think that I'm in love with you" with "George, I think that I'm in love with you." Though, to be fair, Destiny's Child *also* performed at the inauguration, which they got backlash for, but Bush was Beyoncé's former governor, and they were far from being in a position to say "fuck you" to a Republican president lest they end up like the Dixie Chicks, and I don't want to live in that dystopian *Sliding Doors* alternate universe where Destiny's Child turned down Bush and we don't have present-day Beyoncé.

The girl-next-door act didn't do much for Jessica's weak album sales. Plus, she couldn't really dance, and her singing was fine at best (though you'd never know it from the way she attacked a mic while performing, like she was possessed by the Holy Ghost). That all changed once she and her boyfriend Nick Lachey, of the boy band 98 Degrees,* got married. They

---

* Despite no one ever picking them over *NSYNC or BSB, everyone mostly admitted the members of 98 Degrees were hotter than anyone in those groups. BSB were old men. *NSYNC were twinks. And 98 Degrees had Equinox bodies.

launched an MTV reality series, *Newlyweds: Nick and Jessica*, where Jessica played up the stereotype that she was a dumb blonde and laughed all the way to the bank while she became a household name for moments like when she wondered if a can of Chicken of the Sea tuna had fish or chicken in it: "Is this chicken, what I have, or is this fish? I know it's tuna, but it says chicken."

Meanwhile, her younger sister, Ashlee, was launching her own solo career and filmed the making of *Autobiography* for her own reality series, *The Ashlee Simpson Show*. Ashlee's show was the much superior reality show, not relying on Jessica and Nick's saccharine marriage and sitcom-esque plots, but instead showing her struggling with problems with her vocal cords, breaking up with her boyfriend Josh Henderson, and dating Ryan Cabrera, and season two dealt with the fallout from her infamous *Saturday Night Live* performance on October 23, 2004, when the vocals for a different song began playing as she was set to sing the song "Autobiography." She did a very awkward jig on the stage, and the show quickly went to a commercial break. If this had been during the height of social media, it would've made Lana Del Rey's disastrous first *SNL* performance look masterful by comparison.

But to me, there was always something about Ashlee that made her appealing. Maybe it came from having a younger sister who had perfect grades in school who I was always being compared to, but Ashlee seemed more interesting than the blond, perfectly packaged Jessica. Not that "Irresistible" (the So So Def Remix, duh) didn't slap, but Ashlee produced three banger albums: *Autobiography*, *I Am Me* (which produced the perfect pop singles "L.O.V.E." and "Boyfriend"), and a mostly unknown third album, *Bittersweet World*, that Timbaland and Chad

Hugo* put their whole foot in. "Outta My Head (Ay Ya Ya)," "Little Miss Obsessive," "Boys"? But wow, what a moment. A moment that *I* will never forget.

The media always tried to position Ashlee as the messy sister in comparison to Jessica, but one thing I'll tell you is that for several summers in high school I worked at Summerfest, an annual music festival in Milwaukee. My friend Kori used to drive me home from work, because I didn't have a driver's license in high school, after we worked the tickets for the main-stage concerts.

On the night of Jessica Simpson's Reality Tour in 2004, the concert was barely at half capacity. Our bosses told us to let anyone into the venue who wanted to, regardless of whether they'd bought a ticket to see Jessica. A month later, while driving me home, Kori turned on her car and it started loudly playing Ashlee Simpson's "Pieces of Me." She looked to me, embarrassed that she'd forgotten to take the CD out and that I'd just discovered she loved Ashlee Simpson. I quickly assuaged her embarrassment by loudly singing along to the song, and we were both shouting the chorus, "Oooh, it's as if you know me better than I ever knew myself!" as she drove me home. Ashlee Simpson will always be that bitch. And she told us back then, even when people called her music a "guilty pleasure." As she said on "Shadow," her song about having to compete with Jessica's fame, "Mother, sister, father, sister, mother, everything's cool now."

I found a way to get back at Sawyer. It was our senior year and he had to pick someone to succeed him in Conclave. His

---

* Part of the R&B group and production duo the Neptunes alongside Pharrell Williams. He's also part of their group N.E.R.D., which produced one of the best R&B albums of the 2000s, *In Search Of . . .*

candidate, Parker, was running against a friend of mine, Logan, who had absolutely no shot at winning. He didn't even seem like he was serious about student government; he was just running for the position because it was something to do. And that's when I decided I would finally beat Sawyer at something. While Sawyer was spearheading Parker's campaign, I decided to take on Logan's. Despite never having run an election before, I had campaigned for homecoming court and was voted onto it with Kori as my date. She was one of my best friends at the time, and I hadn't come out to her, but she *clearly* knew I was gay and was sweet enough to hold my hand at the dance as we entered for homecoming court.

Though I'd campaigned hard, I lost to a senior who told everyone that he'd get a flaming skull tattoo on his arm and reveal it when he won. When he won, he ripped off his sleeve and showed everyone at the dance his tattoo. Honestly, with that kinda dedication, he deserved to win. But I had a lust for winning ever since then and repeat viewings of the Reese Witherspoon film *Election.*

My first tactic was to promote Logan in the school paper, but since the *Flambeau* barely came out twice a year, I volunteered to moderate the debate between Parker and Logan. Ethically, this was probably dubious, made even worse when I proceeded to make sure I mispronounced Parker's name every time I asked him a question and made sure to ask him the hardest questions submitted by our classmates. And then, just to make sure that Logan really *would* win, I put extra votes in the ballot box. Somehow, Logan *still* lost, which probably means even *he* probably voted for Parker when it was all said and done. I'd lost yet *another* thing to Sawyer, but thank God we were finally graduating and I would never, ever have to see or think about him again.

The next spring, after I'd had my first gay experience and came out at Loyola University Chicago, I returned home for spring break to tell several of my close friends that I was gay. I struggled with trying to soften it by saying I was bi first, but then I realized that wouldn't be even remotely believable. So I came out to several of my friends, and they all took it well. Maybe a little *too* well. No one was surprised that I was gay. And to make matters worse, they had more exciting news to share with me anyway. Sawyer, the charismatic, singing, dancing, perfect-student, student-president star of every single theater production, had come out.

And everyone was absolutely *shocked* because Sawyer didn't seem gay. Or, at least, he didn't seem like a faggot, like me. After finally getting over my hatred of Sawyer . . . he had to go steal my coming-out moment. I found a weird irony in the fact that the very summer Tom Cruise saved cinema post-COVID with *Top Gun: Maverick* was the same summer that Nicole Kidman's campy "we come to this place for magic" AMC commercial became an online phenomenon. Two people who once had a relationship and then became pitted against each other were now back in each other's orbits.

It's rumored that Cruise didn't attend the 2023 Oscars because he didn't want to run into Kidman, who presented at the ceremony, but within that Hollywood ecosystem, they'll always be intertwined in each other's lives somehow. Like me and Sawyer, who heard through a mutual friend once that I'd jokingly referred to him as my "high school nemesis" on my podcast. It wasn't by name, but with enough context clues, it was pretty easy to figure out if you'd gone to school with either of us. We've actually become better friends than we were in high school, when he thought we were genuinely good friends and I just resented him, because the smoke and mirrors are gone. He knows how I felt about him, which was through no fault of his own. I was dealing with my own insecurities and needed someone to blame them on. And he had his own insecurities, clearly, because he was also closeted during our entire high school tenure. There's almost something poetic about us both being closeted, scared teenagers who finally let go of that fear once we were free of our high school prisons.

Time would reveal that Sawyer hadn't actually lost my copy of *Moulin Rouge!* He found it when he was packing to go to Yale for college, and he returned the DVD. When I asked him what he thought about it, he said, "Enh. It kinda sucked."

Actually, maybe I was right to hate him.

> I don't know her.
> —MARIAH CAREY, 2001

· · · · ·

THE EMANCIPATION OF ME

Marilyn Monroe would've loved the internet. Not just because the internet has routinely attributed quotes to her that there's no evidence of her ever saying, like "I'm selfish, impatient, and a little insecure. I make mistakes, I'm out of control, and at times hard to handle. But if you can't handle me at my worst, you sure as hell don't deserve me at my best,"* but because she was born Norma Jeane Mortenson in 1926, and by 1946, she was going by the stage name Marilyn Monroe and had transformed herself into a blond bombshell. She had that in common with most of the stars who'd gone to Hollywood and changed their names: Kirk Douglas, Audrey Hepburn, Rock Hudson, Jamie Foxx, Whoopi Goldberg.

Since Hollywood began, we've been sold fantasies crafted to appeal to our innate desires. Whether they be names that made small-town girls and boys sound larger than life or "exotic" or nonwhite actors who wanted to increase their chances of success, Hollywood is all about selling the fantasy. Which is what the internet has become, particularly to people looking for that other innate human desire: love.

I remember the first time I saw the concept of internet dat-

---

* These are basically the lyrics to Ashlee Simpson's "Pieces of Me" anyway, but as I've said already, she's never been recognized for the poet she is.

ing. It was in an old episode of *The X-Files* that I somehow managed to watch despite it not being a show I was allowed to watch. The 1995 episode "2Shy" was about a monster who preyed on lonely women he met online, women who were overweight and shy and terrified of "disappointment. Rejection. The usual round of suspects." The concept of most episodes of *The X-Files* involved people who were murdered, or bewitched, or had something else paranormal happen to them, in a small American town. Echoes of *Twin Peaks* existed in the series in how it was deliciously nonlinear. Most of the episodes were "monsters of the week" where FBI agents Fox Mulder (David Duchovny) and Dana Scully (Gillian Anderson) investigated some weird phenomenon—murdered circus performers, a man who could squeeze through the smallest of crevices, a string of women giving birth to children with tails, Kathy Griffin attempting to act, etc.

But there were some episodes that contributed to the overall "mythology" of the show, which somehow involved Mulder's sister being abducted by aliens, and Scully's eggs being harvested, and aliens that shape-shifted, and it truly never made any sense, not even in the series finale, where creator Chris Carter attempted to explain everything. The show existed as a series of weird moments that you'll forget ever happened or they'll be stuck in your mind forever.

It's been posited by many that much like video killed the radio star, the internet killed *The X-Files*. When it returned with a slew of new episodes in 2016, fourteen years after the original series ended, it was an exercise in futility. Yes, the episodes were awful, but they also tried to exist in a world that no longer existed. Weird shit that happens in small towns used to be passed along by word of mouth, morphing into urban legends you weren't sure were real. By 2016, anything odd happening in a small town was probably already filmed and uploaded to social media before Mulder and Scully could even book their flights. But that was fine, because I didn't experience *The X-Files* until my adulthood, so the small-town horrors never scared me (except for "Home," that hillbilly-incest episode, because that shit is creepy as hell). But the ones that did scare me were the ones that involved technology.

"Wetwired" is about the government sending signals through TV broadcasts and driving people into a frenzy, which was basically Fox News during the Trump presidency. "Kill Switch" has AI fucking with shit, which is basically the reality we're living in now. And then there's the aforementioned "2Shy," which is all about preying upon people by using the anonymity granted to you by the internet. We kind of know more about one another than we'd ever want to know, but at the same time, how much do we really know about anyone?

One interesting phenomenon I've noticed that has happened since 2020 is the disappearance of a lot of people from social media. Was it a confrontation with the mundanity of life that made people realize that the version of themselves they were presenting online was at odds with who they were, and they couldn't find a way to return to it? Even post-pandemic posting aside, do people tell the truth on dating apps or hookup apps?

In a 2017 interview for Shondaland.com, bell hooks discusses some of her books on relationships, including *All About Love* (side note: If someone recommends this book to you, find out how much bell hooks they've read, because if it's *only* this book, then RUN!) and *The Will to Change: Men, Masculinity, and Love*. She says, "Accepting someone as they are may mean also that you have to accept that they can't be what you want them to be and I think that's really hard for us. We want to make people be what we want them to be."

That has never seemed truer than in the concept of internet dating—we change small details about who we are, and we contact people because they're attractive to *us*, even if we can see the criteria in their dating profile excludes us. I don't even particularly care about people who state their racist or otherwise-discriminatory preferences on apps anymore, because why would you want to pursue someone who has no interest in you? That's a sometimes-easy thing for me to think, but it's not something that was on my mind the first time I found myself using the internet for sex.

After graduating high school and moving to Chicago to attend Loyola University, I was finally able to come out. After all, one of my high school best friends, Luke, was my roommate, and he'd successfully managed to come out our junior year, and the world didn't end for him. But for me, coming out still spelled the end of mine.

Maybe it was because I'd traded one prison for another, this one entirely of my own making. I was gone from my heteronormative Catholic high school, and now people were fulfilling that unspoken promise of coming out once they hit college. There were gay kids everywhere on campus because, well, duh. Also, I was majoring in English and minoring in theater (the minor quickly became a major sophomore year, after a women's literature class made me drop my English major because my professor, in retaliation against the athletes who were attempting to coast in her course, instituted daily pop quizzes about our reading—I was trying to coast too!), but all of the gay kids at college pretty much looked like all the athletic white boys I'd gone to high school with. Once again, because I wasn't comfortable with myself or how I looked, I didn't see a world where I would come out and be just like the other gays on campus. So, I retreated to the internet to find gay people to connect with, people who I could potentially charm with my wit and a single photo of me at my fittest.

The first men who responded to me without me having to message them first on Gay.com, the website where I eventually found my first gay hookup experience, were all white and older. Now that I'm in my thirties, I can see the predatory nature of white men in their late thirties and forties hitting on an eighteen-year-old college student.

But I had my picture hidden to keep anyone on campus from finding my profile, and most of these men didn't want to show a photo either. They were "discreet," which usually meant that they were kind of ugly and knew that showing anyone their real face might turn someone off. Luckily for me, I had just the right amount of low self-esteem to let myself be hit on by Quasimodo if he so chose to message me. One of those Quasimodos—actually, that's being extreme, because I honestly can't remember what the man even looked like—got me to meet up with him.

I left my dorm in the middle of the night and hopped onto the Red Line train at Loyola and took it to the Sheridan stop. It was a cold February in Chicago, and I remember freezing in a light jacket and a scarf and a skullcap, my typical outfit at the time once I'd fallen into realizing Fall Out Boy was my favorite band. I soon arrived at this man's apartment, a man who I had lied to about my sexual history when in fact I'd never even hooked up with another person besides the one girl I'd "dated" in college.

Hannah was a sweet girl from a small town in Wisconsin, to whom you would probably say, "Oh, of course," if you were ever to meet her. We were in one of the same theater classes together, and by the end of the first semester, I was increasingly worried about the fact that people might be catching on to the fact that I was gay. I never talked about anyone I dated, I never seemed to express interest in anyone, so it was of the utmost importance that I find a girlfriend. Or a beard, rather, because even the idea of kissing Hannah stressed me out. I asked her out one day after class, which is shocking to me because I've never been that direct with asking anyone out for the entirety of my life.

I can't remember any of the dates I took Hannah on, but I think one of them was to the Grand Lux Café (the Cheesecake Factory's "fancier" spin-off), the finest of dining for Loyola students at the time, and once we watched *Zoolander* in her dorm. I had only barely kissed Hannah at this point, and I could see that she was probably hoping that we'd at least *try* to approach first base that night.

And I might've forced myself to, if it weren't for the fact that she didn't laugh at *Zoolander* once. Granted, the 2001 moderate box office hit had the unfortunate timing of being released post-9/11 (another victim of that tragedy was *Glitter;* never forget) with a plot to assassinate a president, but it's still incredibly hilarious. When Hannah proclaimed the movie was "stupid," I told her it was over and walked out of her dorm. To this day, I truly do believe it was the fact that she hated *Zoolander* that made me leave and not because I couldn't muster the effort to make out with a woman for half an hour. At the end of the day, all we have is our taste.

When I arrived at this stranger's home off the Sheridan stop, the only thing I remember is that his mouth tasted like sea salt the first time he kissed me and that his half-shaven beard rubbing against my chest made me feel uncomfortable. I remem-

ber the *Late Show with David Letterman* was muted on the TV in
his bedroom and that the hookup didn't even last long enough
for for the *Late Late Show with Craig Ferguson* to begin.

I remember that I came quickly when he sucked my dick,
the first time I had ever felt that sensation not from my right
hand. I remember that his dick tasted like saltwater. For the
longest time, I thought all penises tasted the same until somewhere around my late twenties, when I realized that I *did* enjoy
giving head with the right penis. I was no longer scared of the
dick, as Lil' Kim had prophesized, but I really didn't like the
taste of it.

The first thing I did after leaving the man's apartment was
call Jamal, one of my friends in the theater department. Jamal
and I had become quick friends, mostly because he seemed to
be living a double life that I envied. He was born and raised in
Chicago and not out to his family, but he was out on campus.
He was the only Black gay person I had encountered in my life
besides my uncle Bill, and not only did he fascinate me, but also
he was the first out gay person I'd developed a crush on. Plus,
we were working in close proximity together, as we were both
the assistant stage managers on a production of *Sweeney Todd*.

I had dived headfirst into stage management, even though I
have never been on time for anything in my life, because high
school had already shown me (or so I'd thought) that acting
was not my forte. In my mind, telling Jamal about my first gay
hookup was a way for me to get closer to him. If he knew I was
gay, if he knew that I wanted to be okay with it just like him,
then maybe he'd start to see me as a romantic option.

What occurred was that I had my introduction into how
much people in theater and also gay people love gossip. After I
told Jamal everything about my first encounter with a man, he
hugged me and said, "Welcome to the club." That was a Friday.

By the time Monday rolled around, Jamal (who was stage managing *Godspell* at the same time as his *Sweeney Todd* duties) had told the entire cast of *Godspell* at a cast party that weekend, which had then spread to every gay person on campus.

I remember walking into Damen Dining Hall and being met with knowing grins from two of my classmates who knew I had "come out" over the weekend. I hadn't come out; I'd been outed. When I confronted Jamal about it, he insisted that "everyone knew" I was gay anyway, so there wasn't a big deal in people knowing about it. I've never been fazed by people speculating about the sexualities of celebrities online, because one thing I know from my four years at Loyola is that bored college students do that with their classmates. Once everyone had confirmation that I was gay, they moved on to a new target who they were all waiting to come out.

I will admit I did not react to this in an adult way. Jamal, it turned out, was only out to the theater department. Even on campus, he maintained that he was straight, particularly with one student he had a crush on who didn't know he was gay. So, I stole Jamal's phone one night at rehearsals and sent that student a text telling them Jamal was in love with them. This prompted a two-year feud between us that, in true gay fashion, exploded when we were both working on *The Laramie Project* my sophomore year of college. The story does have a sweet ending, though: We eventually ended up being roommates when we both moved to New York.

Now that I was out on campus, it didn't particularly change anything about my life except that now I added my photo to my Gay.com profile and was also using Craigslist and Manhunt to find more older men to hook up with. Some of them I found hot, some of them I was barely attracted to, but I'd finally found a set of gay men who did find me attractive who weren't just looking for a version of the white, athletic boy I'd grown up with in Milwaukee. But I wasn't out in my everyday life, which included a job at Borders on Michigan Avenue.

Borders was a book megastore that was Barnes & Noble's main competition for decades. Having worked at both Barnes & Noble and Borders, it's easy to see why the latter failed, while I still find myself perusing Barnes & Noble when I have some time to kill. Borders thought it was too big to fail, but it *did* fail. Though I hated pimping that damn e-reader the Nook, which Barnes & Noble created, it was also part of the company's plan to expand beyond a brick-and-mortar store. Borders outsourced all its digital orders to Amazon while Barnes & Noble created their own online store.

Plus, there were far too many damn CDs and DVDs at Borders and a bajillion copies of any book you could ever want. Sometimes it would be annoying when Barnes & Noble didn't have a book you wanted, but you could order it quickly via their online store. It made people start using the online store at home when they didn't want to venture into the physical store. When you didn't want to go into a Borders, you just bought a book on Amazon. It is a sad loss, however, because one thing Borders had going for it was that it was *chic*. On average, the staff at any given Borders was always going to be hotter than that of any given Barnes & Noble. Plus, it was one word. It rolled off the tongue and made you feel the same kind of sexy as the Olsen twins when they're whispering "prune" while posing for a photograph. No one was ever turned on by me working at Barnes & Noble. Meanwhile, I was introduced to the concept of cruising at Borders.

Cruising involves the act of making eye contact with another man in public and then finding the most convenient place to have sex. It can happen in a bar, on a subway train, in a park, or even in a Borders, where I was cruised for the first time. I worked at Borders beginning in December 2004, the end of my first semester at Loyola, and continued working there throughout my second semester, where I found my first adult gay mentor, Richard. Richard was an older co-worker who stanned Mariah Carey. It was with him that I felt most comfortable in the "real world" that wasn't the Loyola campus. He was an adult I didn't have to watch my mannerisms around or worry about how my voice sounded when speaking to him.

When I say Richard was a Mariah Cary stan, he was a *stan*. He was a Lamb! Which is a name Carey calls her fanbase. I liked Mariah Carey well enough; I'd gone to see *Glitter* in theaters! But aside from a few of Mariah's older singles like "Honey" or "Fantasy," which played in regular rotation on VH1's block of classic videos, I had not yet peeped Carey's game. I assure you I am now as die-hard a Lamb as they come now, but in the spring of 2005, before *The Emancipation of Mimi* had been released, I was not by any means listening to Mariah on any regular basis.

In January, Carey released the first single from *The Emancipation of Mimi*, "It's Like That," and it became one of her biggest hits in years, since her career had taken a hit after an erratic public appearance on *TRL* and the aforementioned failure of *Glitter*. Richard couldn't stop talking about Carey's imminent comeback in the break room while I was trying to finally read *The Corrections* (I never finished it, and I never started *Freedom**

---

* I will never get over the out-of-body experience of white bookstore customers approaching me to ask, "Do you know where I can find *Freedom*?"

or *Purity*, but I did buy them like an idiot who thinks I'll ever finish a Franzen novel*). When the full album dropped, he played it constantly on the store's speakers and in the break room.

I liked the first single well enough, but I was *obsessed* with the Shakespearean-level lyric "them chickens is ash and I'm lotion."† However, Kelly Clarkson had just released *Breakaway* and Ashanti had released *Concrete Rose*, two albums I still listen to on the regular, so my mind was musically occupied elsewhere. That is, until "We Belong Together" dropped. As I said, most people considered Carey's career over. She was no longer the number one Billboard Hot 100 queen—no, really, she released an album in 1998 simply titled *#1's,* and it featured all thirteen of her number one singles at the time.

She released *#1 to Infinity* in 2015, updating the album to include the fact that she by then had earned eighteen number one Billboard hits and launched a Vegas residency of the same name, where she performed all eighteen of her number ones. In 2019, "All I Want for Christmas Is You" (originally released in 1994), became her nineteenth number one. But "We Belong Together" was a massive hit; it ratcheted to number one and spent fourteen weeks at the top of the charts. Richard's prophesized comeback was actually coming, and I was becoming a full-on Lamb. I might've thought my coming-out was telling my friend that I'd sucked a dick for the first time, but it was publicly embracing Mariah Carey at work alongside Richard

---

* I have read his essay collection, *How to Be Alone*, however, because who can't finish an essay collection? Most of my friends I give my book to, probably.

† Mariah Carey's wordplay is unmatched. Who else is rhyming "rendezvous" with "all up in my business like a Wendy interview"? Wendy Williams, her longtime nemesis, to be exact.

that made it very clear to all of our co-workers at Borders that I, too, was an out gay man.

On the occasion of the release of *The Emancipation of Mimi*, there was a hot, older British gentleman who entered the store to pick up the album, and he asked me to help him find it and the latest Bret Easton Ellis novel, *Lunar Park*. Which, coincidentally, is how I first discovered who Ellis was and subsequently one of my favorite novels, *Less than Zero*.

Once he'd grabbed the books he wanted, he asked me where the closest restroom was, and I pointed it out. As he headed toward the bathroom, he turned back to stare at me intently. I could feel my face going flush, my jeans tightening. This was the first time another man had expressed sexual interest in me in public, not from behind a computer screen. I followed him into the bathroom, and we gave each other hasty blow jobs in a handicap stall. Finally, I could rap along to Lil' Kim with honesty! I was scared of the dick no longer.

And the Oscar goes to . . . *Crash.*

—JACK NICHOLSON, THE 78TH ACADEMY AWARDS (2006)

. . . . .

DECEMBER 9, 2005

In December 2005, Ang Lee's gay film classic, *Brokeback Mountain* (should've beat *Crash* for Best Picture, but it's not a movie that makes people feel "good" for absolutely nothing like *Crash*), was released in theaters and my friends made plans to see it opening night. By that point, I had settled into being an out gay man on campus.

I didn't have a fake ID, so I'd yet to visit a gay bar, but in the summer of 2005, I briefly began casually hooking up with someone for the first time—and they were a classmate of mine, not someone who was expecting AARP mailings at home. I told my friends about hooking up with our classmate Levi. I even made out with that Levi in public at a party. I was *out*. And I wasn't afraid of being out anymore, of doing publicly gay things, because nothing could hurt me anymore.

As I put on my peacoat (now that I was gay, I was wearing much better winter coats already) and rushed out of my dorm to meet my friends (I was running late, as usual), I stepped into the crosswalk when the light turned green, and within seconds a car slammed into me. I tumbled onto the hood of the car, then slid off in a daze, but I didn't fall to the pavement. I stood there, stunned, catching my balance. And then the car pulled away. It was a fucking hit-and-run. A few passersby approached me and asked if I was okay, if they needed to call the police, if

I'd seen the license plate number of the person who hit me. I mumbled something about "being late to *Brokeback Mountain*," then hurried on my way. I remember being proud that I told strangers I was going to see *Brokeback Mountain*.

Later, the realization set in that I probably should've skipped the fucking movie, laid my ass on the pavement, and collected a check from the bitch who hit me with their car and drove off.

I was officially gay, but it turns out I was also an idiot.

Acknowledgments

·····

This book would not exist without the listeners and subscribers of *Keep It,* the pop culture podcast I've hosted for the past seven years. I owe so much of this book to years of debate and conversation with one of the smartest pop culture minds I know, my *Keep It* co-host Louis Virtel. Thank you to my previous co-hosts, Kara Brown and Aida Osman. Thank you to Jon Favreau, Jon Lovett, Tanya Somanader, and Tommy Vietor for inviting me into the Crooked family in 2017. Thank you to Ana Marie Cox for introducing me to them in the first place on your podcast *With Friends Like These.* Thank you to my current producers Chris Lord, Kennedy Hill, and Kendra James. Thank you also to Megan Patsel, Claudia Sheng, Rachel Gaewski, Evan Sutton, Matt DeGroot, David Toles, Kyle Seglin, and Charlotte Landes for helping to produce *Keep It* each week. And thank you to my former producers Corinne Gilliard, Caroline Reston, and Ceej Polkinghorne for shaping the show's voice over the years.

But this book *really* wouldn't be a damn thing without the warmth, feedback, and vision of my editor, Jamia Wilson. I've worked with a lot of editors, but you're the first one who made me feel like I could write an entire book long before the final product materialized. And thank you to everyone at Random House, especially Miriam Khanukaev, for helping us throughout the entire journey. Also thank you to production editor

Andy Lefkowitz, managing editor Rebecca Berlant, interior designer Elizabeth Rendfleisch, production manager Kevin Garcia, publicist Vanessa DeJesus, marketer Ayelet Durantt, copy chief Dennis Ambrose, and cover designer Mimi Bark.

Thank you to Erin Malone, who pushed me to write this book long before she became my agent at WME. Thank you also to my manager, Kailey Marsh, for getting me signed at WME in the first place, and for always believing in my writing career amidst missed deadlines and years of unfinished ideas.

Thank you to Adam Falkner, the only friend I let read early essays of *Pure Innocent Fun* before my editor read them. Thank you also to Juan A. Ramírez for the endless drinks and dinners I've been late to while working on this book, and all of the theater I've been your plus-one to.

Thank you to former colleagues at the short-lived reboot of MTV News (2015–2016, R.I.P.) whose work I reread copiously when I felt like I didn't know how to write anymore, but especially that of Doreen St. Félix.

Thank you to New York City, Los Angeles, Miami, Fire Island Pines, Bogotá, Cartagena, London, and Amsterdam, where I wrote this book over the course of two years. Thank you to Beyoncé and the Renaissance World Tour, for which I finally finished the first draft so I could enjoy the concert without thinking about my unfinished book.

Thank you to my most important group chats who've heard me talk about this book more than anybody should have ever had to: Word on the Street, Niggas in Amsterdam, The Boys, The Council, and Heauxchella.

Thank you to my family! Gran, who this book is dedicated to, as well as my mom, my sister, my niece, my granddad, and my extended family in Milwaukee and Elkhart. I love you all.

Some Background

. . . . .

INTRODUCTION: ON CHUCK KLOSTERMAN

Klosterman, Chuck. *Fargo Rock City: A Heavy Metal Odyssey in Rural North Dakota*. Scribner. May 22, 2001.

———. *Sex, Drugs, and Cocoa Puffs: A Low Culture Manifesto*. Scribner. August 26, 2003.

LeMay, Matt. "Liz Phair: *Liz Phair* Album Review." Pitchfork. June 24, 2003.

WHITE BOYS

Nicholson, Amy. *Tom Cruise: Anatomy of an Actor*. Phaidon Press. July 28, 2014.

Peretz, Evgenia. "Being Tom Cruise." *Vanity Fair.* January 2002.

Shakespeare, William. *Julius Caesar.* 1599.

NO WATCHING *THE SIMPSONS*

Bush, George H. W. 1992 State of the Union Address. January 28, 1992.

Moret, Jim. "Jerry Springer the 'Ringmaster' of His Domain." CNN Showbiz Today. November 18, 1998.

Springer, Jerry, and Laura Morton. *Ringmaster!* St. Martin's Press. November 1, 1998.

Tucker, Reed. "Ay, Caramba! We're Old, Man!" *New York Post.* July 22, 2007.

Zoller Seitz, Matt, and Alan Sepinwall. *The Sopranos Sessions.* Abrams Press. January 8, 2019.

BEING STEVE URKEL

Baldwin, James. *The Amen Corner: A Play.* Dial Press. 1954.

——. *Blues for Mister Charlie: A Play.* Dial Press. 1964.

Blakemore, Erin. "The Latchkey Generation: How Bad Was It?" *JSTOR Daily.* November 9, 2015.

Brooks, Tim, and Earle F. Marsh. *The Complete Directory to Prime Time Network and Cable TV Shows: 1946–Present.* Ballantine Books. October 16, 2007.

Fuller, Linda K. *The Cosby Show: Audiences, Impact, and Implications.* Praeger. September 30, 1992.

Moore, Demi. *Inside Out: A Memoir.* Harper Perennial. September 24, 2019.

Smith, Will. *Will.* Penguin Press. November 9, 2021.

DAMN, GINA!

Berkman, Meredith. "Martin Lawrence Makes the Jump from TV to Film." *Entertainment Weekly.* February 4, 1994.

Curran, Colleen. *Whores on the Hill.* Vintage. May 10, 2005.

Rosenberg, Howard. "A New Low on the Taste Meter." *Los Angeles Times.* December 15, 1993.

HERO TO ZERO

Crichton, Michael. *Jurassic Park.* Knopf. November 20, 1990.

Lescher, Mary E. *The Disney Animation Renaissance: Behind the Glass at the Florida Studio.* University of Illinois Press. November 22, 2022.

MTV News. "Whitney Houston Reminisces About '80s Music on MTV." MTV. January 1, 2001.

OPRAH RUINED MY LIFE

American Heart Association. "Report: Tobacco Industry Continuing Decades-Long Targeting of Black Communities, Women, Youth with Menthol Products." AHA Newsroom. October 4, 2022.

Blum, David. "Hollywood's Brat Pack." *New York.* June 10, 1985.

Capparell, Stephanie. "How Pepsi Opened Door to Diversity." *The Wall Street Journal.* January 9, 2007.

Estes, Adam Clark. "A Brief History of Racist Soft Drinks." *The Atlantic.* January 28, 2013.

Miller, Sam, and Rochelle Herman. *Jared from Subway: Catching a Monster.* Investigation Discovery. March 6, 2023.

Spitzner, Eric. "The MH Interview: Jared Fogle." *Men's Health.* April 5, 2013.

Taylor, LaTonya. "The Church of O." *Christianity Today.* April 1, 2002.

I'M NOT DARIA

Armstrong, Lance. *It's Not About the Bike: My Journey Back to Life.* Putnam. May 22, 2000.

Twain, Mark. *The Adventures of Huckleberry Finn.* Chatto & Windus. December 10, 1884.

Willman, Chris. "The Dixie Chicks Take on Their Critics." *Entertainment Weekly.* April 24, 2003.

Zoller Seitz, Matt, and Alan Sepinwall. *The Sopranos Sessions.* Abrams Press. January 8, 2019.

THE WINNER TAKES IT ALL

American Idol. "Top 6 Perform." Fox. April 27, 2004.

———. "Top 6 Results." Fox. April 28, 2004.

Fessenden, Ford, and John M. Broder. "Examining the Vote: The Overview; Study of Disputed Florida Ballots Find Justices Did Not Cast the Deciding Vote." *The New York Times.* November 12, 2001.

Harris, Zelda, and Marian Lebor. "Golda Meir Teacher Takes Fourth Graders to Europe." *Wisconsin Jewish Chronicle.* May 14, 2008.

Klosterman, Chuck. "ABBA 1, World 0." *Eating the Dinosaur.* Simon & Schuster. October 20, 2009.

Moore, David W. *How to Steal an Election.* Hachette. September 28, 2006.

FAN FICTION

Bushnell, Candace. *Sex and the City.* Atlantic Monthly Press. August 12, 1996.

Gumbel, Andrew. "The Truth About Columbine." *The Guardian.* April 16, 2009.

King, Michael Patrick. "No Ifs, Ands or Butts." *Sex and the City.* HBO. July 9, 2000.

Nussbaum, Emily. "Difficult Women." *The New Yorker.* July 22, 2013.

Tolentino, Jia. "Candace Bushnell Is Back in the City." *The New Yorker.* February 16, 2022.

WHOOPI

Ebert, Roger. "Whoopi Goldberg: 'The Color Purple.'" *Chicago Sun-Times.* December 15, 1985.

The Oprah Winfrey Show. "Whoopi Goldberg and 25 Years Later: *The Color Purple* Reunion." ABC. November 15, 2020.

Schulman, Michael. *Her Again: Becoming Meryl Streep.* HarperCollins. April 26, 2016.

MONDAYS ARE A BITCH

Bellafante, Ginia. "Feminism: It's All About Me!" *Time.* June 29, 1998.

Feitelberg, Rosemary. "Nam June Paik's Futuristic Thinking Still Rings True." *Women's Wear Daily.* November 26, 2022.

Heath, Chris. "The Emotional Odyssey of Angelina Jolie: Heartbreaker, Tomb Raider, and Bride of Billy Bob." *Rolling Stone.* July 5, 2001.

Jackson, Michael R. *A Strange Loop.* Theatre Communications Group. January 19, 2021.

Lauerman, Kerry. "In 'Glittering' Return, Paglia Lets Loose." Salon. October 10, 2012.

Morris, Wesley. "Why Is Everyone Always Stealing Black Music?" *The New York Times Magazine.* August 14, 2019.

Pure Soap. "Camille Paglia." E! 1994.

Ribowsky, Mark. *The Supremes: A Saga of Motown Dreams, Success, and Betrayal.* Da Capo Press. April 27, 2010.

Robinson, Lisa. "It Happened in Hitsville." *Vanity Fair.* December 13, 2008.

Scott, Melody Thomas, with Dana L. Davis. *Always Young and Restless: My Life on and off America's #1 Daytime Drama.* Diversion Books. August 18, 2020.

Sheff, David. "Playboy Interview: John Lennon & Yoko Ono." *Playboy.* January 1981.

I USED TO BE SCARED OF THE DICK

Bozza, Anthony. "'N Sync: Weird Scenes Inside the Glitter Factory." *Rolling Stone.* March 30, 2000.

DeKnight, Steven S. "Dead Things." *Buffy the Vampire Slayer.* February 5, 2002.

Hedegaard, Erik. "Backstreet Boys: The Boys in the Bubble." *Rolling Stone.* December 14, 2000.

hooks, bell. "Hardcore Honey: bell hooks Goes on the Down Low with Lil' Kim." *Paper.* May 1997.

———. *Rock My Soul: Black People and Self-Esteem.* Washington Square Press. January 6, 2004.

Powers, Devon. "Lil' Kim: The Notorious K.I.M." *PopMatters.* June 27, 2000.

Samuels, Allison. "A Whole Lotta Lil' Kim." *Newsweek.* June 25, 2000.

Spanos, Brittany. "'N Sync vs. Backstreet Boys: Remembering the Nineties' Definitive Boy-Band Rivalry." *Rolling Stone.* March 23, 2018.

A VIRGIN WHO CAN'T DRIVE

Ellis, Brett Easton. *Less than Zero*. Simon & Schuster. 1985.

Jackson, Reggie. "A White Utopia: How a Segregated Milwaukee Created the Arrogance of Suburbia." *Milwaukee Independent*. December 16, 2020.

BRING IT

Ebert, Roger. "Bring It On." *Chicago Sun-Times*. August 25, 2000.

Wickman, Kase. *Bring It On: The Complete Story of the Cheerleading Movie That Changed, Like, Everything (No, Seriously)*. Chicago Review Press. December 6, 2022.

THE EMANCIPATION OF ME

Bereola, Abigail. "Tough Love with bell hooks." *Shondaland*. December 13, 2017.

Ellis, Brett Easton. *Lunar Park*. Knopf. August 16, 2005.

Knowles, Chris, and Matt Hurwitz. *The Complete X-Files: Behind the Scenes, the Myths, and the Movies*. Insight Editions. November 11, 2008.

Phillips, Brian. "In the Dark." *Grantland*. September 9, 2013.

DECEMBER 9, 2005

Ebert, Roger. "Love on a Lonesome Trail." *Chicago Sun-Times*. December 15, 2005.

Coates, Ta-Nehisi. "Worst Movie of the Decade." *The Atlantic*. December 30, 2009.

About the Author

Ira Madison III is the host of Crooked Media's pop culture podcast *Keep It*. He has written for *GQ*, *New York* magazine, *Interview*, MTV News, and *Cosmopolitan*, among other publications. *Nylon* named him one of the "most reliably hilarious and incisive cultural critics writing now." His television writing credits include *Uncoupled*, *Q-Force*, *Nikki Fre$h*, and *So Help Me Todd*. He has appeared on *The Late Show with Stephen Colbert*, *Watch What Happens Live with Andy Cohen*, *The Wendy Williams Show*, and the second season of Netflix drama *You*. He lives in New York City.

About the Type

This book was set in Dante, a typeface designed by Giovanni Mardersteig (1892–1977). Conceived as a private type for the Officina Bodoni in Verona, Italy, Dante was originally cut only for hand composition by Charles Malin, the famous Parisian punch cutter, between 1946 and 1952. Its first use was in an edition of Boccaccio's *Trattatello in laude di Dante* that appeared in 1954. The Monotype Corporation's version of Dante followed in 1957. Though modeled on the Aldine type used for Pietro Cardinal Bembo's treatise *De Aetna* in 1495, Dante is a thoroughly modern interpretation of that venerable face.